IMPROVING YOUR SERVE

The Art of Unselfish Living

BIBLE STUDY GUIDE

From the Bible-teaching ministry of

Charles R. Swindoll

INSIGHT FOR LIVING

Chuck graduated in 1963 from Dallas Theological Seminary, where he now serves as the school's fourth president, helping to prepare a new generation of men and women for the ministry. Chuck has served in pastorates in three states: Massachusetts, Texas, and California, including almost twenty-three years at the First Evangelical Free Church in Fullerton, California. His sermon messages have been aired over radio since 1979 as the *Insight for Living* broadcast. A best-selling author, Chuck has written numerous books and booklets on many subjects.

Based on the outlines and transcripts of Chuck's sermons, the study guide text is co-authored by Lee Hough, a graduate of the University of Texas at Arlington and Dallas Theological Seminary. He also wrote the Living Insights sections.

Editor in Chief:
Cynthia Swindoll

Coauthor of Text:
Lee Hough

Assistant Editor:
Wendy Peterson

Copy Editors:
Deborah Gibbs
Cheryl Gilmore
Glenda Schlahta

Designer:
Gary Lett

Publishing System Specialist:
Bob Haskins

Director, Communications Division:
Deedee Snyder

Manager, Creative Services:
Alene Cooper

Project Supervisor:
Susan Nelson

Print Production Manager:
John Norton

Unless otherwise identified, all Scripture references are from the New American Standard Bible, © The Lockman Foundation 1960, 1962, 1963, 1968, 1971, 1972, 1973, 1975, 1977. Used by permission. Scripture taken from the Holy Bible, New International Version, Copyright © 1973, 1978, 1984 International Bible Society, used by permission of Zondervan Bible Publishers. Other translations cited are *The Living Bible* [LB] and *J.B. Phillips: The New Testament in Modern English* [PHILLIPS].

An effort has been made to locate sources and obtain permission where necessary for the quotations used in this book. In the event of any unintentional omission, a modification will gladly be incorporated in future printings.

ISBN 1-57972-000-5
Printed in the United States of America.

CONTENTS

1. This study is for chapter 1 in the book *Improving Your Serve: The Art of Unselfish Living* (Waco, Tex.: Word Books, 1981) titled "Who, Me a Servant? You Gotta Be Kidding!" There is no cassette for this message.

2. This message is in the cassette series but was not included in the book.

3. This message is in the cassette series but was not included in the book.

INTRODUCTION

More than ever before, selfishness has become a way of life. We think about ourselves, watch out for ourselves, and talk about ourselves, and we defend ourselves when confronted with criticism. Ours is indeed a "me-first" generation that finds itself in a confused tailspin, smug and preoccupied with its own needs, yet desperately lonely, isolated, and cold. We are losing touch with one another, running faster even though we have lost our way.

These lessons offer straight talk and solid, biblical answers on how to live an unselfish life . . . how to be a people-helper, how to serve rather than always expecting to receive, how to give rather than striving to get and keep.

It will seem strange, perhaps, because this message is so seldom heard . . . so rarely demonstrated today. But it is desperately needed!

Isn't this what Jesus Christ modeled and proclaimed? Wasn't He the One who said He didn't come to be served, but to serve and to give His life as a ransom? And when He had the opportunity to take charge and do things His way, wasn't He the One who obeyed the Father, serving Him in authentic humility?

My prayer is that you will sense in these lessons an unusual amount of encouragement to improve your serve as you live in and cope with a world that needs these messages more than ever in history.

Chuck Swindoll

PUTTING TRUTH
INTO ACTION

K nowledge apart from application falls short of God's desire for His children. He wants us to apply what we learn so that we will change and grow. This study guide was prepared with these goals in mind. As you go through the following pages, we hope your desire to discover biblical truth will grow as your understanding of God's Word increases, and that you will be encouraged to apply what you've learned.

To assist you in your study, we've included a section called 🍵 **Living Insights** at the end of each lesson. These exercises will challenge you to study further and to think of specific ways to put your discoveries into action.

There are many ways to use this guide—in personal devotions, group studies, discussions with friends and family, and Sunday school classes. And, of course, it's an ideal study aid when you're listening to its corresponding "Insight for Living" radio series.

To benefit most from this study guide, we would encourage you to consider it a spiritual journal. That's why we've included space in the **Living Insights** for recording your thoughts and discoveries. We hope you'll return to those sections often for review and encouragement as you continue to grow in your walk with Christ.

Lee Hough
Coauthor of Text
Author of Living Insights

IMPROVING YOUR SERVE

The Art of Unselfish Living

Chapter 1

WHO, ME A SERVANT? YOU GOTTA BE KIDDING!

Selected Scriptures

What do you think of when you hear the word *servant*? Maybe someone who is taken for granted and used like an appliance? Maybe someone with limited options and even less respect, expected to plod along without feeling, thought, or purpose other than to do the master's bidding?

Obviously, most people would not consider the title "servant" a glamorous one. Certainly not one we're anxious to list on our résumés. *Master* of something or other, yes, but *servant*? Absolutely not.

Is it any wonder, then, why people are confused by Bible expositors who link the terms *servant* and *leader* together as being the Christian ideal? How can a will-less servant lead, or what powerful leader would obediently wait on others? The two terms seem completely antithetical.

But are they?

If we accept the world's definition of *servant*, then, yes, it would be the opposite of *leader*. If, however, we redefine those words according to their use in God's Word, we'll discover a whole new meaning and likeness between two seemingly opposite words. Authentic servanthood, the life Jesus modeled, transcends our ideas of petty servility to introduce something new, something pure, something powerful. If we learn how to practice His kind of service, it will transform not only the way we lead but also the way we live.

A Foundational Perspective on Servanthood

The biblical concept of servanthood is founded in God's ultimate goal for all Christians, mentioned in Romans 8:28–29.

1

And we know that God causes all things to work together for good to those who love God, to those who are called according to His purpose. For whom He foreknew, He also predestined *to become conformed to the image of His Son,* that He might be the first-born among many brethren. (emphasis added)

The Father's aim is to reproduce Christ's image in each of us. But what, exactly, is that image? What does it look like? Jesus provides two clues in His explanation of His purpose for coming.

"For even the Son of Man did not come to be served, but to serve, and to give His life a ransom for many." (Mark 10:45)

Serving and *giving*—these are two chief qualities that, when practiced, help mold us into the image of Christ—an image whose contours are shaped by the daily sacrifices of an unselfish life. But that pleasing profile won't happen overnight. Like an athlete's muscles, it takes time and hard work to develop them. It's a process, one that involves a constant struggle between our natural lust to selfishly rule and the godly desire to selflessly serve.

Serving versus Ruling

Even Christ's own disciples, men who actually lived with the greatest example of servanthood ever, struggled to overcome their desire to rule rather than serve. Matthew 20 records the embarrassing occasion when a mother's request exposed the Twelve's selfish ambitions to reign with Jesus in His kingdom.

Then the mother of the sons of Zebedee came to Him with her sons, bowing down, and making a request of Him. And He said to her, "What do you wish?" She said to Him, "Command that in Your kingdom these two sons of mine may sit, one on Your right and one on Your left." . . . And hearing this, the ten became indignant with the two brothers. (vv. 20–21, 24)

Can you guess why the other ten became indignant? Of course you can . . . in their hearts, each one of them had already claimed one of the thrones next to Jesus for himself. No way were they going to give up the most prestigious seats in the new kingdom—

2

not without a fight!

Perceiving the root of the conflict, Jesus pulled the disciples aside to spell out the sharp contrast between His way of ruling and the world's.

> "You know that the rulers of the Gentiles lord it over them, and their great men exercise authority over them. It is not so among you, but whoever wishes to become great among you shall be your servant, and whoever wishes to be first among you shall be your slave; just as the Son of Man did not come to be served, but to serve, and to give His life a ransom for many." (vv. 25–28)

"Whoever wishes to be first among you shall be your slave." Read on and you'll notice that no one, not even the good Mrs. Zebedee, was interested in continuing the battle for the best seat. Jesus' definition of ruling had turned their whole way of thinking upside down.

We shouldn't judge them too harshly, however, because we, too, struggle with the temptation to rule instead of serve. Even in many churches today the focus is more on superstars than on servants. Celebrity-status leaders are sought after to draw and entertain crowds because we've gone back to the world's standard of associating greatness with popularity. To guard against such a mistake, we need to remember that there is only one leader, one head of the church—Jesus Christ (see Col. 1:15–18). Now that doesn't mean churches are to operate without any form of government, just that all Christians, leaders and lay people alike, are to function with a servant's heart. It's the *attitude* that's most important.

Paul: Servanthood Modeled

Outside of the Lord Jesus Himself, perhaps the finest model of servanthood to ever live was a devout Jew from Tarsus named Saul. Once known as a Pharisee of Pharisees, a ruthless persecutor of Christians, Saul became the apostle Paul after his conversion and spent the rest of his life passionately serving Christ and others.

Let's take a close look at three distinguishing qualities of servanthood that set him apart as one of God's greatest leaders.

Transparent Humanity

Listen to Paul's words to the Corinthians:

3

> And when I came to you, brethren, I did not come
> with superiority of speech or of wisdom, proclaiming
> to you the testimony of God. For I determined to
> know nothing among you except Jesus Christ, and
> Him crucified. And I was with you in weakness and
> in fear and in much trembling. (1 Cor. 2:1–3)

Was the Apostle being self-effacingly modest? No, actually he was being transparently honest about something even popular opinion confirmed.

> For they say, "His letters are weighty and strong, but
> his personal presence is unimpressive, and his speech
> contemptible." (2 Cor. 10:10)

Paul had weaknesses, lots of them. And like a servant, he openly admitted his needs rather than trying to hide his humanity behind a false bravado. Servants are transparent like that. There's a genuineness about them that guards against a pretentious, self-inflated attitude.

Genuine Humility

Going back to Paul's first letter to the Corinthians, we find another distinctive trait of servanthood mirrored in his admission that

> my message and my preaching were not in persuasive
> words of wisdom, but in demonstration of the Spirit
> and of power, that your faith should not rest on the
> wisdom of men, but on the power of God.
> (1 Cor. 2:4–5)

Paul's concern was that others would be impressed, not with his ability, but with God's power. That's authentic humility. He deliberately drew people's attention away from himself and to the Lord.

When people follow image-conscious leaders, however, it's the leader who's exalted, not the true Head of the church. So how can we discern whether someone has a servant's heart? Here are a couple of revealing tests of humility. First, ask yourself, Does this person manifest a nondefensive spirit when confronted? Is he or she willing to be accountable? And second, Does this individual exhibit an authentic desire to help? Is he or she in touch with the needs of others? The humble servant always looks for ways to help and care.

Absolute Honesty

A third crucial characteristic of a servant is revealed in Paul's statements regarding the integrity of his ministry.

> Therefore, since we have this ministry, as we received mercy, we do not lose heart, but we have renounced the things hidden because of shame, not walking in craftiness or adulterating the word of God, but by the manifestation of truth commending ourselves to every man's conscience in the sight of God. (2 Cor. 4:1–2)

> For our exhortation does not come from error or impurity or by way of deceit; but just as we have been approved by God to be entrusted with the gospel, so we speak, not as pleasing men but God, who examines our hearts. (1 Thess. 2:3–4)

Paul's transparency and humility, combined with his honesty, created a ministry free of ulterior motives, hidden agendas, hypocrisy, duplicity, and political games. He was open to scrutiny and dedicated to the truth and to following through on his word. All these are signs of an honest servant.

A Challenge

Before going on to the next chapter, pause to consider the three traits of a servant in the light of your own life. Think about what qualities your life reflects, as compared to the serving and giving that characterized the lives of Jesus Christ and the apostle Paul. None of us, of course, will measure up perfectly to Christ's image; but the good news is that God's ready to improve your serve. The question is, are you?

📖 *Living Insights* STUDY ONE

For most of us, what we need as we begin our study on servanthood is *not* an archaeological dig into the pre-Flood roots of the word *servant* or any esoteric explanations of what it means to serve and give. All too often believers hide behind such academic explorations as a way of keeping the subject at arm's length. Oh sure, they can always rattle off impressive technical truths about the word, but they're talking about something they're completely detached from, something they've never known personally.

Let's get personal. That's what is needed if this study is to have any impact in the way we serve and give to others. But how? How do we take the biblical truths studied thus far and for the rest of this guide about servanthood and bring them down into our own lives? One way is through meditation.

Remember God's promises in Psalm 1?

> How blessed is the man who . . .
> [delights] in the law of the Lord,
> And in His law he *meditates* day and night.
> And he will be like a tree firmly planted by streams
>   of water,
> Which yields its fruit in its season,
> And its leaf does not wither;
> And in whatever he does, he prospers.
> (vv. 1–3, emphasis added)

In his excellent book *Spiritual Disciplines for the Christian Life,* Donald Whitney writes:

> The tree of your spiritual life thrives best with meditation because it helps you absorb the water of God's Word (Ephesians 5:26). Merely hearing or reading the Bible, for example, can be like a short rainfall on hard ground. Regardless of the amount or intensity of the rain, most runs off and little sinks in. Meditation opens the soil of the soul and lets the water of God's Word percolate in deeply.[1]

Today, meditate on the biblical truths studied in our first chapter. Memorize a passage, rewrite another in your own words, look deeply into the meaning of still another by emphasizing a different word or phrase each time you repeat it. Ask application-oriented questions, such as these Whitney recommends:

> Does this text reveal something I should believe about God?

1. Donald S. Whitney, *Spiritual Disciplines for the Christian Life* (Colorado Springs, Colo.: NavPress, 1991), pp. 45–46.

Does this text reveal something I should praise or thank or trust God for?

Does this text reveal something I should pray about for myself or others?

Does this text reveal something I should have a new attitude about?

Does this text reveal something I should make a decision about?

Does this text reveal something I should do for the sake of Christ, others, or myself?[2]

If you will approach the biblical truths concerning servanthood through these kinds of meditations, you'll have no problem filling the space provided with personal insights to make you a more transparent, humble, and honest servant.

_____

_____

_____

_____

_____

Living Insights   STUDY TWO

Now that we've given ourselves to meditating on these beginning truths about servanthood, the natural next step is prayer. Meditation fuels prayer, enriches it, makes it personal and passionate.

Allow this prayer taken from Ken Gire's wonderful book *Instructive Moments with the Savior* to guide your meditations into heartfelt prayers. It follows a devotion centered on the classic example of an authentic servant—the Good Samaritan. The end of the prayer has been left open so that you can continue with your own thoughts and words.

Dear Jesus, . . .

As I have traveled down the road to my many

2. Whitney, *Spiritual Disciplines*, p. 56.

responsibilities, how often have I taken a detour around the person in need? How often have I dismissed that need as none of my business?

Forgive me, Lord, for being so concerned about my other commitments that I am unconcerned about my commitment to others. Help me to realize that so much of true ministry is not what I schedule but what comes as an intrusion to my schedule.

Keep my schedule flexible enough, Lord, so that when my path comes across someone in need, I would be quick to change my plans in preference to yours.

Give me a heart of compassion that I may love my neighbor the way the good Samaritan loved his. Give me eyes that do not look away and feet that do not turn to the other side of the road.

Who is my neighbor, Lord?

> Is it the shut-in, stripped of her independence by arthritis, beaten down by the years, hanging on to life by a thread?
>
> Is it the AIDS victim, stripped of a long life, battered by an insidious virus, his life silently flickering away unnoticed in a hospice?
>
> Is it the bag lady, stripped of her home, broken by the hard reality of the pavement, kept alive by the pocket change of a few kind strangers?
>
> Is it the old man on the street, stripped of his dignity, beaten down by alcohol, half-starved as he rummages through a dumpster for his daily bread?
>
> Is it the woman next door, stripped of her happiness, black and blue from a bad marriage, wishing she were dead?
>
> Is it the man down the hall, stripped of his assets, battered by the economy, whose business is bankrupt?

Deep down inside, Lord, my heart knows the answer. I don't even have to ask. These are my neighbors.

Help me to love them.

Deliver me from stillborn emotions, which look at those on the roadside with a tear in my eye but without the least intention of helping them. Impress upon my heart, Lord, that the smallest act of kindness is better than the greatest of kind intentions.

Help me to realize that although I cannot do everything to alleviate the suffering in this world, I can do something. And even if that something is a very little thing, it is better than turning my head and walking away. . . .[3]

3. Ken Gire, *Instructive Moments with the Savior* (Grand Rapids, Mich.: Zondervan Publishing House, 1992), pp. 21–22.

Chapter 2

GOD'S WORK, MY INVOLVEMENT
2 Corinthians 2–4

Going to a large church has its advantages. There are more activities to be involved in, more ministries to benefit from, perhaps nicer facilities to enjoy . . . but it has its drawbacks too. It's easy to feel lost, unnoticed, and unappreciated in a large church. Every Sunday you might sit next to someone you don't know, even if you've attended the church for years. You can feel alienated— even embarrassed. For example, have you ever had the pastor ask everyone to turn and meet their neighbor? You politely introduce yourself, saying, "Welcome, my name is Paul Waters, and I'm glad you've come to worship with us. I don't believe I've ever seen you here before. Are you new?" To which the nice elderly man replies, "No, Paul, I've been an elder in this church since it was founded twenty years ago." "That's nice," you mumble as you slump back in your pew.

Can you imagine what it would be like to belong to a church so large that it conducted *five* services every Sunday, and even then many people were turned away? How does one minister in such a setting? What involvement can we possibly have among such a sea of strangers? These were exactly the conditions and challenges facing the First Evangelical Free Church of Fullerton, California, in the late seventies. An incredible season of expansion took place that brought with it many growing pains for the people who worshiped there.

How did they cope? In this chapter, we'll look at the insights they found in 2 Corinthians—insights from an apostle with an expanding ministry of his own.

Some Background

Beginning with verse 12 of chapter 2, the apostle Paul provides us with several important details concerning his ministry as it was about to grow in ways he'd never dreamed.

> Now when I came to Troas for the gospel of

Christ and when a door was opened for me in the Lord, I had no rest for my spirit, not finding Titus my brother; but taking my leave of them, I went on to Macedonia.

But thanks be to God, who always leads us in His triumph in Christ, and manifests through us the sweet aroma of the knowledge of Him in every place. For we are a fragrance of Christ to God among those who are being saved and among those who are perishing; to the one an aroma from death to death, to the other an aroma from life to life. (vv. 12–16a)

Notice first of all that Paul didn't open the door to ministry—God did (v. 12). Second, the Apostle wasn't satisfied to simply stay in Troas, he "went on" to Macedonia (v. 13). And third, Paul didn't stay in one place forever, he shared the sweet aroma of Christ in "every place" (v. 14).

Changes were entering Paul's life and ministry that really stretched him. The door into Macedonia, modern-day Europe, was one he'd never even knocked on before. To step through it meant leaving the familiar territories of Asia and Palestine—areas he was raised in. He knew the culture, the language, the people. His roots were there. But now the Spirit of God was leading him into something new. So it's only natural, in light of the awesome consequences of his task and the unfamiliarity of the future, for the Apostle to ask, "Who is adequate for these things?" (v. 16b).

The church in Fullerton wondered that same thing. Like Paul, they hadn't opened the door to an expanded ministry, but God did; and it was causing the pews to overflow and the ministry to broaden into unknown territories. How did they remain adequate to minister in the midst of such changes? They followed the Apostle: they "went on"; they were not content to maintain the status quo and instead learned how to become a sweet aroma in "every place." For a closer look at how they accomplished this, here are four practical insights they gleaned from Paul's life and ministry.

Four Facts of Ministry to Be Observed

As great an evangelist as Paul was, we must remember that he was simply a human being like the rest of us, with the same obstacles to overcome. One obstacle he faced, something common to us all, was the challenge of *change*.

Implementing Change Is Difficult

A psychologist once said that the two hardest things to do are to give up something old and to take on something new. For Paul, change meant giving up the ministry in his homeland to take on a new one in cities he'd never evangelized before, like Philippi, Thessalonica, Berea, and Corinth. For the Fullerton church, it meant giving up many of the comforts and traditions of the past to take on traffic jams, overcrowded parking lots, neighborhood resentment, larger Sunday school classes, crowded services, and ruffled feelings among people being shuttled here and there.

Implementing change is difficult; it stretches us, causes friction, and often raises fears that prod us to close doors rather than keep them open. Yet Paul went on to Macedonia. Why? Because he believed that no matter how difficult or how many the changes that lay ahead, God would "always lead [him] in His triumph in Christ" (v. 14). The church of Fullerton could believe no less and so went forward, trusting in His triumphant leading for their expanding ministry.

Becoming Large Is Suspect

Another insight from Paul's ministry that helped the church in its transition is found in verse 17.

> For we are not like many, peddling the word of God,
> but as from sincerity, but as from God, we speak in
> Christ in the sight of God.

In a rare moment, the Apostle pauses to defend himself against being associated with those false apostles who selfishly and dishonestly hawked the gospel for their own profit. Apparently, some people in Corinth had observed his ministry from a distance and falsely assumed that he must be like those other charlatans. Their perception was wrong, of course, but not all that unusual.

We often become suspicious of a ministry—whether it involves an individual, a church, or a parachurch organization—as it expands and moves in new directions. We tend to assume that the ministry is changing for the worse, that it's becoming uncaring, full of itself, money-mad, manipulative, and exploitative. And, no doubt, many individuals and ministries have become just those things as they grew. But growth needn't ruin a ministry if the leaders remain teachable and vulnerable. Sincerity must be the goal, not showmanship (see 4:1–2).

Involving People Is Basic

Knowing that some would undoubtedly interpret his defense of himself as prideful boasting, Paul goes on to say in 3:1–3:

> Are we beginning to commend ourselves again? Or do we need, as some, letters of commendation to you or from you? You are our letter, written in our hearts, known and read by all men; being manifested that you are a letter of Christ, cared for by us, written not with ink, but with the Spirit of the living God, not on tablets of stone, but on tablets of human hearts.

Was the Apostle's ministry simply an ego trip designed to promote him? Of course not, and Paul didn't need anyone's affidavits. The Corinthians themselves were his proof. They knew how he had selflessly poured out his own life to build them up in the faith. They had become living letters of Christ Himself, testifying to the truth that Paul sought to serve, not to be served.

It is important to remember that each of us is a letter of Christ as well—and a letter that's being read. To stay healthy and keep up with the needs brought on by growth, a ministry needs the involvement of all its members. For if we recognize only a few, we deprive others of sharing their part of Christ's story, and our ministry is destined for difficulty. People-worship will result, centered around the performance of a few prima donnas.

Remaining Servants Is Essential

This final fact for ministries to observe takes us back to Paul's original question—"Who is adequate for these things?" (2:16b). Who is adequate to carry out the ministry of God? In answer to this, the Apostle wrote,

> Not that we are adequate in ourselves to consider anything as coming from ourselves, but our adequacy is from God, who also made us adequate as servants of a new covenant, not of the letter, but of the Spirit; for the letter kills, but the Spirit gives life. (3:5–6)

Paul was not adequate in himself to take on the ministry in Macedonia any more than the church in Fullerton was adequate in itself to take on the ministry of a growing congregation. By ourselves, we're all inadequate to handle God's work. But as servants of Jesus Christ, we are made adequate by the work of the Holy Spirit within us. Wherever the Spirit is at work through servants, there will be a vibrant, dynamic life marked by a liberty to grow as God leads (see vv. 6, 17).

Accountability in Ministry

Regardless of the size of our ministries or our churches, Paul reminds us in chapter 4 that we've each been given two things we're accountable for: "we have this ministry" (v. 1), and "we have this treasure" (v. 7). The treasure he's referring to is the glorious gospel of Jesus Christ, which we are to freely share with others. And our ministry? The Greek term for that word means "to serve"— that is what each of us must strive to do in our homes, at work, in our churches, everywhere. Only by becoming a servant of the Lord Jesus Christ can we find the adequacy to fulfill the mission God has planned for us.

🍵 *Living Insights* STUDY ONE

Today, as you look at the local church, something basic, something fundamental to its very nature is vanishing. It seems that fewer and fewer believers arrive Sunday mornings with an attitude like Christ's, one that seeks to serve rather than be served. Instead, more and more of us come wanting, expecting to be entertained— "please me," "serve me," "make me feel good."

Has that attitude crept into your thinking? Have you been coming and going to church each week without ever stopping to consider how you might serve? Perhaps you're already giving. If so, that's wonderful; keep it up! If, however, you're not serving in any capacity, we'd like to encourage you to consider some possibilities. Perhaps one or two from the following list might be ways you've never thought of and would fit your talents and interests. Ignore whichever ones don't apply at your church; and if a way of serving comes to mind that's not on the list, jot it down in the space provided.

Service Possibilities

Helping Hands
Usher ☐
Assisting Senior Adults:
    Active Seniors ☐
    Homebound ☐
    Nursing Help ☐
Assisting Single Parents:
    Baby-sitting ☐
    Big Brother/Sister ☐
General Assistance:
    Home Repairs ☐
    Transportation ☐
    Car Repair ☐

Office Skills/Communications
Information Center Attendant ☐
Tape Ministry ☐
Office Assistant ☐
    (Mailings, Labeling, Copying)
Bulletin Preparation ☐
Newsletter Mailing ☐

Technical Skills/Graphics/Sound
Writer ☐
Artist (Graphic Illustrator) ☐
Photographer ☐
Production:
    Videography ☐
    Multi-image ☐
    Voice-over/Narration ☐
Audiovisual Attendant ☐
Sound/Recording Team ☐
Production Coordinator ☐

Music and the Arts
Library Volunteer ☐
Organist ☐
Pianist ☐
Accompanist ☐
Instrumental Music ☐
    Instrument: _____
Director ☐
Assistant ☐
Resource Person ☐
Hands-on Helper ☐
Special Events Helper ☐
Creative Arts:
    Banners ☐
    Decorations ☐

Set Construction ☐
Costume Seamstress ☐
Dance ☐
Drama ☐
Readers' Theater ☐
Crafts ☐
Flowers ☐

Care and Concern
Food Fund Volunteer ☐
Homeless Ministry ☐
Hospital Visitation ☐
Unwed Mothers ☐
Job Bank ☐
Prison Ministry:
    Assistance ☐
    Outreach ☐
    Housing ☐
    Transportation ☐
Volunteer Care Giver:
    Temporary ☐
    Long-Term ☐
Lay Counseling ☐
Disabilities Ministry ☐

Youth/College Ministry
Adult Ministry Team/Junior High ☐
Adult Ministry Team/High School ☐
College Ministry ☐
    Discipleship Leader ☐

Men's/Women's Ministries
Small Group Bible Study:
    Leader ☐
    Host ☐
    Assistant ☐
Focus on Missions ☐
Special Events ☐
Mentoring ☐
Hospitality Committee ☐

Christian Education
Lead Teacher ☐
Teacher ☐
Substitute ☐
Helper ☐
Secretary ☐
Music ☐
Games/Recreation ☐
Craft/Hobby Teacher ☐

Your Own Ideas

_____   _____

_____   _____

_____   _____

_____   _____

_____   _____

_____   _____

📖 *Living Insights*

In his excellent book *Spiritual Disciplines for the Christian Life*, Donald Whitney writes:

> When God calls His elect to Himself, He calls no one to idleness. When we are born again and our sins forgiven, the blood of Christ cleanses our conscience, according to Hebrews 9:14, in order for us to "serve the living God!" "Serve the Lord with gladness" (Psalm 100:2, NASB) is every Christian's commission. There is no such thing as spiritual unemployment or spiritual retirement in the Kingdom of God.[1]

Even though we are all expected to serve, the question remains, Are we willing to serve? Whitney continues,

> The Israelites knew without a doubt that God *expected* them to serve Him, but Joshua once looked them in the eye and challenged them on their *willingness* to serve: "But if serving the Lord seems undesirable to you, then choose for yourselves this day whom you will serve. . . . But as for me and my household, we will serve the Lord" (Joshua 24:15).[2]

1. Donald S. Whitney, *Spiritual Disciplines for the Christian Life* (Colorado Springs, Colo.: NavPress, 1991), pp. 111–12.

2. Whitney, *Disciplines*, p. 122.

Is Joshua speaking to you? Have you made up your mind whom you will serve, or is the position of servanthood that God has for you still unfilled?

Must have BA in Business or related major. MA preferred. Six figure salary, and perks to the right person.

WANTED: Volunteers for service in the local expression of the Kingdom of God. Must be transparent, humble, and honest. No sense of adequacy required, only a willing heart.[3]

WANTED: Fortune 500 company seeks highly motivated go-getter with ample experience in corporate take over. Applicants must know

---

3. Adapted from Whitney, *Disciplines*, p. 122–23.

Chapter 3

A CASE FOR UNSELFISHNESS
Genesis 3:6–13; Mark 10:42–45

W hat is it that urges me to always do what's best for me, regardless of what's best for others?

What is it that causes you to pout when you don't get exactly what you want?

What is it inside each of us that demands we get whatever we want when we want it?

What is that dark impulse that furiously ignites over even the smallest issue?

Where does the desperate feeling come from that stubbornly refuses to admit any wrongdoing? Where does the obsessive preoccupation with self get its power?

Something is wrong, bent, twisted beneath the smooth surface of our smiles. Something more hideous than any of us dare believe. Yet we can feel its presence; we've seen its destructive power. It's there staring at us in the faces of the dead at Auschwitz; we can see it in the sunken eyes of starving children whose relief food was stolen by greedy warlords; we saw it in the fetid hellholes created for unwanted children in Romania under Nicolae Ceausescu's reign; it's visible everywhere pain and suffering exists. No evil, however brutal, is beyond the imagination of this invisible beast. It has no remorse, no friends, absolutely no respect for anyone's life but its own.

Who or what is this monster, this insatiable demon that incessantly pushes us to promote itself? It is *selfishness*, what the apostle Paul calls our "old self" (see Eph. 4:22; Col. 3:9). Sometimes we curse it; other times we pamper and protect this destructive desire inherited from our parents.

However, selfishness didn't begin simply with our parents. To trace its origin we must go back to an ancient scene pictured for us in the second and third chapters of Genesis, in the Garden of Eden.

Relationship of Adam and Eve: Absence of Selfishness

Eden was paradise, a luxurious garden planted by the Creator Himself. It was to be both a honeymoon suite and home for the newlywed crown of His creation, Adam and Eve. Theirs was an ideal marriage, unblemished by sin. The unique closeness and unity which flourished in the rich soil of that relationship is summed up in the words "And the man and his wife were both naked and were not ashamed" (Gen. 2:25).

Naked, laid bare, open—these words describe not only the physical aspect of their relationship, but the emotional as well. Adam and Eve were completely transparent and at ease in each other's presence. The Hebrew construction of the verse reinforces this idea, suggesting that they were not ashamed with one another. Their conversations, their actions, their emotions, their entire lives were unguarded and absolutely unselfish—until . . .

Results of Sin: Preoccupation with Self

. . . until Adam and Eve ate from the forbidden tree and the honeymoon with God, each other, and innocence ended.

> Then the eyes of both of them were opened, and they knew that they were naked; and they sewed fig leaves together and made themselves loin coverings. (3:7)

Notice what occurred first because of Adam and Eve's sin—their eyes were opened. Suddenly the two became self-conscious, something they'd never experienced before; and with that new awareness came new feelings of shame and embarrassment about their nakedness. No longer could they openly relate to one another in the innocence of a perfectly balanced relationship. An immediate refocusing on self took over that sent both scrambling for something to cover themselves. Selfishness, looking out only for number one, was born . . . and soon it made its presence felt even more strongly.

> And they heard the sound of the Lord God walking in the garden in the cool of the day, and the man and his wife hid themselves from the presence of the Lord God among the trees of the garden. Then the Lord God called to the man, and said to him, "Where are you?" And he said, "I heard the sound of Thee in the garden, and I was afraid because I

was naked; so I hid myself." (vv. 8–10)

In his insightful book *The Trauma of Transparency*, J. Grant Howard takes us behind the scene of Adam's words to reveal the fallen self's pervasive influence.

> Forced out of hiding, Adam stands shamefacedly before his Judge and mumbles his reply. These are the first recorded words of a sinner. Note how he communicates. He mixes truth—"I was afraid"— with half-truth—"because I was naked." The full truth was that he had disobeyed God and thus was aware of his nakedness. He did not level with God. He concealed his act of willfull disobedience instead of openly and honestly confessing it. Adam can no longer function as a completely authentic person.[1]

Adam's newborn selfishness digs in to defend itself even more stubbornly when God asks the probing question,

> "Who told you that you were naked? Have you eaten from the tree of which I commanded you not to eat?" And the man said, "The woman whom Thou gavest to be with me, she gave me from the tree, and I ate." (vv. 11–12)

Instead of admitting his own sin, Adam is quick to point out Eve's culpability. But he doesn't stop there. He even tries to include the Lord in his widening circle of blame by reminding Him that it was He who brought Eve to him in the first place!

When asked about her role, Eve responds by pointing the finger of fault at the serpent (v. 13)—implying, of course, like Adam, that this whole mess was the Lord's fault because He created the serpent. What twisted rationalization sin drives us to!

First Adam and Eve hid, then they blamed, cutting a pattern of self-protection humanity has followed ever since. Why? Because with sin comes selfishness. It's a congenital disease of the soul to which no one is immune (compare Rom. 5:12–21).

No one, that is, except God's Son.

Born of a virgin, Jesus was delivered into this world completely

---

1. J. Grant Howard, *The Trauma of Transparency* (Portland, Oreg.: Multnomah Press, 1979), p. 30.

sinless. And it's by His life and example that the beauty of unselfishness, lost in Eden, can be restored in our own lives.

Realm of Servanthood: Unselfishness Restored

Selfishness can give way to unselfishness, but it will never come naturally. Only Christ can empower us to replace our tendencies to hide and blame with His humble desire to serve. Even with His help, however, change won't be easy. As Christ explained to His disciples, it will take nothing short of a complete turnaround in our thinking about serving.

> And calling them to Himself, Jesus said to them, "You know that those who are recognized as rulers of the Gentiles lord it over them; and their great men exercise authority over them. But it is not so among you, but whoever wishes to become great among you shall be your servant; and whoever wishes to be first among you shall be slave of all. For even the Son of Man did not come to be served, but to serve, and to give His life a ransom for many." (Mark 10:42–45)

Years later, this same Christlike attitude of serving and giving is exactly what the apostle Paul encouraged the saints in Philippi to emulate.

> Do nothing from selfishness or empty conceit, but with humility of mind let each of you regard one another as more important than himself; do not merely look out for your own personal interests, but also for the interests of others. Have this attitude in yourselves which was also in Christ Jesus. (Phil. 2:3–5)

Consider the contrast between Paul's counsel and the world's, as illustrated by J. B. Phillips' altered version of the Beatitudes.

> Happy are the pushers: for they get on in the world.
> Happy are the hard-boiled: for they never let life
>   hurt them.
> Happy are they who complain: for they get their
>   own way in the end.
> Happy are the blasé: for they never worry over their
>   sins.

Happy are the slave-drivers: for they get results.
Happy are the knowledgeable men of the world: for
    they know their way around.
Happy are the trouble-makers: for people have to
    take notice of them.[2]

Not a bad portrait of selfishness, is it? We see it every day—at
work, on the news, in crowded stores and streets. Its ubiquitous
presence is felt by everyone. What a striking difference, then, when
lost and hurting people see a servant of Christ who is not quarrel-
some but

> kind to all, able to teach, patient when wronged,
> with gentleness correcting those who are in opposi-
> tion, if perhaps God may grant them repentance
> leading to the knowledge of the truth, and they may
> come to their senses and escape from the snare of
> the devil, having been held captive by him to do
> his will. (2 Tim. 2:24b–26)

Road of Servanthood: Traits of Selflessness

Summed up, there are three traits that will plant our feet firmly
on the road to servanthood. The first is *giving*. A servant is someone
who's willing to be vulnerable instead of hidden and unapproach-
able. He or she releases rather than keeps, has an open hand rather
than a tight fist, is compassionate instead of calloused. The second
is *forgiving*. Servants seek to understand instead of casting blame.
The third is *forgetting*. Servants release themselves and others from
guilt, in place of holding a grudge.

🍺 *Living Insights*   STUDY ONE

Take a moment to reflect on your day yesterday. Could you build
a case for your own unselfishness based on the way you treated your
roommate or spouse before you went to work?

How about the way you drove to work? What about while you
were at the office? What evidence could you marshal forth to convince a jury of your servantlike attitude toward your boss and your

2. J. B. Phillips, *Your God Is Too Small* (New York, N.Y.: Macmillan Co., 1961), p. 92.

coworkers? What personal sacrifices did you make in order to put someone else's interests before your own?

When you came home yesterday, how did you demonstrate to your children or parents that they were more important than yourself?

Are there any witnesses—a business associate, a waitress, a needy stranger, a neighbor—who could testify on your behalf regarding a specific act of selfless giving?

Do you think you've got a case? Make it. But remember, only hard evidence, verifiable facts, are admissible. Good intentions won't stand up in court. Still have a good case?

If you were to get a second chance, say, if your trial was postponed until the day after tomorrow, what changes in your attitude and behavior could you plan so that you'd have enough evidence to guarantee a conviction of servanthood in the first degree?

A Case for Unselfishness

_____

_____

_____

_____

_____

_____

_____

_____

🍵 *Living Insights* STUDY TWO

Perhaps preparing your case in the previous Living Insight forced you to examine some concrete examples of selfishness in your life. That's good, really, because until we are willing to recognize our own selfishness—not just that of Adam and Eve—talk of becoming a servant will be just that, talk.

Let's take a step beyond talking by spending some time in confession. Servanthood is born out of a broken and contrite heart (Ps. 51:17). But selfishness will do everything it can to keep you from bowing the knee and confessing it as sin before the throne of

23

God. Your pride will try to get you to cover up and make excuses for it, just like Adam and Eve. But we must utterly forsake both pride and selfishness. "Do *nothing* from selfishness . . . ," Paul writes, "but with humility of mind let each of you regard one another as more important than himself" (Phil. 2:3, emphasis added).

Cultivate that humility of mind now by rooting out your selfishness through confession. Begin by letting the words of David break open pride's seal on your heart.

> Search me, O God, and know my heart;
> Try me and know my anxious thoughts;
> And see if there be any hurtful way in me,
> And lead me in the everlasting way.
> (Ps. 139:23–24)

Chapter 4

THE SERVANT AS A GIVER
(PART ONE)
2 Corinthians 8:1–5

An editorial cartoon once depicted these four words, apparently chiseled out of granite, as a great shrine surrounded by a multitude of arm-waving worshipers. They form the altar of self-preoccupation before which all humanity instinctively kneels. From this altar flow popular teachings that have tickled our ears for centuries. For example,

> Epicureanism: "Be sensuous, enjoy yourself!"
> Materialism: "Be satisfied, hoard for yourself!"
> Humanism: "Be strong, believe in yourself!"
> Pride: "Be superior, promote yourself!"

The emphasis may vary, but the basic refrain always remains the same—yourself, yourself, yourself.

Isn't There a Better Way?

Is it any wonder, then, why our world is swollen with so much greed, so much conflict, and so much cruelty? If all 5.3 billion of us are pushing and shoving with religious fervor to find fulfillment at the altar of self-indulgence, nothing but friction and fighting will ever result.

There is a better way, however—one that can free us from our bondage to the monotonous mantra of "I, me, mine, myself." That way is found in the model and message of Jesus Christ, summed up in the words "Be a servant—think of others."

Think of others? Sure, but always after I've taken care of number one, right? Wrong. As the apostle Paul unequivocally admonishes,

> Do nothing from selfishness or empty conceit, but with

25

humility of mind let each of you regard one another as more important than himself; do not merely look out for your own personal interests, but also for the interests of others. Have this attitude in yourselves which was also in Christ Jesus. (Phil. 2:3–5)

That attitude permeates practically every page of the Scriptures. Take a moment to immerse yourself in the following passages, absorbing the spirit of a true servant.

Jesus, knowing that the Father had given all things into His hands, and that He had come forth from God, and was going back to God, rose from supper, and laid aside His garments; and taking a towel, He girded Himself about. Then He poured water into the basin, and began to wash the disciples' feet, and to wipe them with the towel with which He was girded. . . .

And so when He had washed their feet, and taken His garments, and reclined at the table again, He said to them, "Do you know what I have done to you? You call Me Teacher and Lord; and you are right, for so I am. If I then, the Lord and the Teacher, washed your feet, you also ought to wash one another's feet. For I gave you an example that you also should do as I did to you. Truly, truly, I say to you, a slave is not greater than his master; neither is one who is sent greater than the one who sent him. If you know these things, you are blessed if you do them." (John 13:3–5, 12–17)

"For who is greater, the one who reclines at the table, or the one who serves? Is it not the one who reclines at the table? But I [Jesus] am among you as one who serves." (Luke 22:27)

For we do not preach ourselves but Christ Jesus as Lord, and ourselves as your bond-servants for Jesus' sake. (2 Cor. 4:5)

For the love of Christ controls us, having concluded this, that one died for all, therefore all died; and He died for all, that they who live should no longer live for themselves, but for Him who died and rose again on their behalf. (2 Cor. 5:14–15)

For you were called to freedom, brethren; only do not turn your freedom into an opportunity for the flesh, but through love serve one another. (Gal. 5:13)

Be devoted to one another in brotherly love; give preference to one another in honor; not lagging behind in diligence, fervent in spirit, serving the Lord; rejoicing in hope, persevering in tribulation, devoted to prayer. (Rom. 12:10–12)

Now some might read these verses and mistakenly conclude that the Christian attitude is one of inferiority. But nothing could be further from the truth, as we see in these words written by the apostle Paul.

For I consider myself not in the least inferior to the most eminent apostles. . . .

I have become foolish; you yourselves compelled me. Actually I should have been commended by you, for in no respect was I inferior to the most eminent apostles, even though I am a nobody. (2 Cor. 11:5; 12:11)

Authentic humility is in no way the equivalent of groveling servility. The servanthood Paul modeled wasn't motivated by feelings of inferiority but by the gracious love of Christ (see 2 Cor. 5:14–15). Therefore, he could reach out to others, overflowing with Christ's unconditional love and power, and minister competently, freely, and with the same love he had been given.

What Are the Basics?

As we mentioned in the closing of the previous chapter, a servant has three essential qualities—he or she must be *giving*, *forgiving*, and *forgetting*. We'll be studying those last two more closely in subsequent chapters; for now, let's focus our attention on four principles for giving gleaned from 2 Corinthians 8.

How Should Servants Give?

The context in which we find our four principles involves Paul's

27

efforts to collect money for needy Christians in Jerusalem. According to commentator David K. Lowery,

> The Corinthians, hearing about "the collection," asked Paul what part they might have in it (cf. 1 Cor. 16:1). Paul instructed them concerning these arrangements (1 Cor. 16:2–3). Good intentions had not been translated into fruition, however, so Paul asked Titus to look into the matter. . . .
> Titus had found the Corinthians in need of an encouraging word which Paul delivered in chapters 8–9 of this letter.[1]

As a way of motivating the Corinthians, the Apostle holds up the example of the Macedonian believers, who, although hurting financially themselves, gave liberally to support their brothers and sisters in Christ in Jerusalem.

> Now, brethren, we wish to make known to you the grace of God which has been given in the churches of Macedonia, that in a great ordeal of affliction their abundance of joy and their deep poverty overflowed in the wealth of their liberality. For I testify that according to their ability, and beyond their ability they gave of their own accord, begging us with much entreaty for the favor of participation in the support of the saints, and this, not as we had expected, but they first gave themselves to the Lord and to us by the will of God. (2 Cor. 8:1–5)

The first principle for how a servant should give, inferred from the Macedonians' example, is a subtle one. So subtle you might have missed it altogether—but then, you were supposed to.

Anonymously

Look carefully at the first verse again, and you'll notice that not one specific church is named for its giving. The Apostle simply says, "the churches of Macedonia." No individual or group is praised for giving. There is no highlighting the highest donors for others to

---

1. David K. Lowery, "2 Corinthians," *The Bible Knowledge Commentary*, New Testament ed. (Wheaton, Ill.: Scripture Press Publications, Victor Books, 1983), p. 572.

ooh and ahh over. Apparently, no one put conditions on his or her contributions, saying they would give—if—the saints in Jerusalem would carve their names in the pastor's podium. No, they simply gave, anonymously.

Is this the attitude we have when we give? Are we willing to support others without getting any recognition in return? "I wonder," mused Ruth Harms Calkin in a poem she wrote by that title.

> You know, Lord, how I serve You
> With great emotional fervor
> In the limelight.
> You know how eagerly I speak for You
> At a women's club.
> You know how I effervesce when I promote
> A fellowship group.
> You know my genuine enthusiasm
> At a Bible study.
>
> But how would I react, I wonder
> If You pointed to a basin of water
> And asked me to wash the calloused feet
> Of a bent and wrinkled old woman
> Day after day
> Month after month
> In a room where nobody saw
> And nobody knew.[2]

True servants are content to give without anybody seeing or knowing except the Father in heaven (see Matt. 6:1–4). In fact, they prefer anonymity, being embarrassed when others try to put their names in lights.

Generously

A second principle modeled by the Macedonians is sacrificial giving. Paul says they "overflowed in the wealth of their liberality" to the point of even giving "beyond their ability" (2 Cor. 8:2b, 3b). Now that's generosity. Especially in light of the fact that these people were experiencing "a great ordeal of affliction" and "deep poverty" themselves (v. 2).

---

2. Ruth Harms Calkin, "I Wonder," in *Tell Me Again, Lord, I Forget* (Elgin, Ill.: David C. Cook Publishing Co., 1974), p. 23. Used by permission of Tyndale House Publishers.

Commentator William Barclay wrote,

> It is not always those who are most wealthy who are
> most generous; often those who have least to give
> are the most ready to give. As the common saying
> has it, "It is the poor who help the poor," because
> they know what poverty is like.[3]

Regardless of whether you're rich or poor, remember that a
servant isn't simply someone who gives; rather, he or she is someone
who gives generously. And that includes giving of our time, our
talents, and our hearts as well.

Voluntarily

The third commendable principle we can draw from the Macedonians is that giving should be done willingly; nobody should have
to twist our arm.

> I can testify that they did it because they wanted to,
> and not because of nagging on my part. They begged
> us to take the money so they could share in the joy
> of helping the Christians in Jerusalem. (vv. 3b–4 LB)

Paul encouraged this same spirit of voluntary giving a little later
in the same letter by saying,

> Let each one do just as he has purposed in his heart;
> not grudgingly or under compulsion; for God loves
> a cheerful giver. (9:7)

When was the last time you heard of someone begging to help
someone else? Isn't much of our giving today done under the coer-
cion of preachers who pressure with a few tear-jerking pleas? Whatever happened to the servant who cheerfully volunteered to give
without having to be asked? Such giving requires reaching out and
being in touch with the needs of others, rather than hiding in hope
that no one will ask for our help.

Personally

This final principle deals with how the Macedonians "first gave
themselves to the Lord and to us" (8:5, emphasis added). Notice the

---

3. William Barclay, *The Letters to the Corinthians*, rev. ed., The Daily Study Bible Series
(Philadelphia, Pa.: Westminster Press, 1975), p. 229.

order: first to the Lord, then to others. Elton Trueblood once commented,

> The man who supposes that he has no time to pray or to reflect, because the social tasks are numerous and urgent, will soon find that he has become fundamentally unproductive, because he will have separated his life from its roots. . . .
>
> The emphasis upon inner development, when fully considered, turns out to be the most unselfish of enterprises, because, as we live for one another, the best we can give is ourselves.[4]

By giving themselves to the Lord first, the Macedonians unselfishly prepared the way for their personal involvement in meeting the needs of their fellow Christians in Jerusalem. In the same way, putting the Lord first in our lives is a prerequisite to giving ourselves personally.

This kind of giving is not something that can be done at arm's length or *in absentia*—either with the Lord or with the people we're supposedly trying to help. It means getting close, interacting, opening up, learning what it means to be doers of the Word and not merely hearers who delude themselves (James 1:22).

🍵 *Living Insights* STUDY ONE

Have you ever been poor?

I don't mean the kind of poor where we compare our three-bedroom homes to our neighbors' five-bedroom homes and think, "Boy, are they rich." Not that kind of poor.

I don't mean the kind of poor where we tell our friends how strapped we are financially, all the while carrying membership cards to our favorite clubs, spas, and amusement parks.

I don't mean the kind where we complain about how we don't have any money when we have thousands in our savings and retirement accounts. None of that. I'm talking about real poverty— empty stomachs and empty pockets—the kind of meager existence

---

4. Elton Trueblood, *The New Man for Our Time* (New York, N.Y.: Harper and Row, Publishers, 1970), pp. 60, 79.

the Macedonians experienced. Have you ever been that poor?

The truth is, the only poverty many of us will ever know concerns our giving, not our living. Our standard of living probably far exceeds the Macedonians', but is our giving below the poverty line? Has our selfishness impoverished our witness as giving servants of Christ? If so, that's *true* poverty.

Have you ever been that poor?

☕ *Li̲vi̲ng* I̲n̲sights̲

In his commentary on 2 Corinthians, Philip E. Hughes writes:

> So far from enjoying conditions of material wealth and prosperity which would have enabled them to subscribe without discomfort, [the Macedonians] gave in circumstances of the severe testing of affliction and rock-bottom poverty. Their own impoverishment was extreme; they were already, as it were, scraping the bottom of the barrel. But, regardless of this, they gave with joy and liberality. The effectiveness of Paul's description of this situation is enhanced by the use of a double paradox: in the midst of testing *affliction* the Macedonian Christians knew an abundance of *joy*, and their rock-bottom *poverty* they had used as an opportunity for abounding in the *wealth* of generosity. In this they had shown themselves to be truly Christlike.
>
> The example of the Macedonians is a practical proof that true generosity is not the prerogative of those who enjoy an adequacy of means. The most genuine liberality is frequently displayed by those who have least to give. Christian giving is estimated in terms not of quantity but of sacrifice. Thus the widow who cast her two mites into the treasury gave more than all the others together, because they gave "of their superfluity", at no real cost to themselves, whereas she gave "all that she had, even all her living" (Mk. 12:41ff.).[5]

5. Philip Edgcumbe Hughes, *Paul's Second Epistle to the Corinthians* (Grand Rapids, Mich.: William B. Eerdmans Publishing Co., 1962), p. 288.

How often is your giving, whether financial or personal, marked by the sacrificial generosity of the widow and the Macedonians? What practical proofs from your own life could you cite to support your answer?

_____

_____

_____

_____

Take some time, perhaps days or even several weeks, to pray and seek God's heart about this. Also, if you're married, consider this with your spouse and children. When you come to a decision, write down what you plan to do. Your present giving may be fine, or perhaps you feel a change is in order. Whatever the situation, record it here to help keep yourself on track.

_____

_____

_____

_____

_____

Chapter 5

THE SERVANT AS A GIVER
(PART TWO)
2 Corinthians 8:7–12; 9:6–8

As we learned in our last lesson, servants have a passion for giving without recognition, without reservation, and without restriction. Such an unselfish attitude, however, doesn't come cheaply. Let's continue our study in 2 Corinthians and find out some of the specific costs involved in cultivating a lifestyle of giving.

How Much Does Giving Cost Us?

In chapter 8, remember, the apostle Paul held up the Macedonians' generous giving as a model for the Corinthians to follow. Having done that, he now encourages them to carry through their good intentions toward the needy Christians in Jerusalem and give generously. As we look closely at Paul's earnest exhortation, we'll find that to give as he recommends will cost the Corinthians in at least three different ways.

It Costs a Thorough Self-Evaluation

The first price tag is tucked away in verses 6–9.

> We have urged Titus, who encouraged your giving in the first place, to visit you and encourage you to complete your share in this ministry of giving. You people there are leaders in so many ways—you have so much faith, so many good preachers, so much learning, so much enthusiasm, so much love for us. Now I want you to be leaders also in the spirit of cheerful giving.
>
> I am not giving you an order; I am not saying you must do it, but others are eager for it. This is one way to prove that your love is real, that it goes beyond mere words.
>
> You know how full of love and kindness our Lord Jesus was: though he was so very rich, yet to help you he became so very poor, so that by being poor he could make you rich. (vv. 6–9 LB)

Paul's words urge the Corinthians to probe deeply into their own hearts and wrestle with some key issues concerning giving. Four of these issues in particular can help all of us better evaluate our own giving.

First, *seek the objectivity of another person* (v. 6). To conduct a thorough examination of our giving, we all need, at times, the impartial insights of another person. Titus was that person for the Corinthians. Apparently, he had helped initiate their support for the church in Jerusalem on a previous visit. Now he was needed again, to see their collection through to completion—just as each of us also needs a Titus from time to time who will point out the blind spots in our serving that keep us from being generous givers.

Second, *ask hard questions of yourself* (v. 7). Paul exhorted the Corinthians to abound in their giving the same as they abounded, for example, in their faith, knowledge, and love. By comparing the one to the others, the Apostle wanted the readers to ask themselves the hard question regarding why they overflowed in all these areas except generosity.

We, too, must ask hard questions of ourselves: I abound in this, that, and that over there, but what about my giving? No amount of other gifts minimizes our need to abound in generosity.

Third, *examine your motives* (v. 8). Paul doesn't command the Corinthians to give; rather, he beseeches them to, according to the love they have for the Lord and their fellow brothers and sisters in Christ. By asking in this way, the Apostle gently prompts them to consider their motive for giving—whether it is, in fact, love or perhaps something else.

Every thorough examination of our giving must include motives: Am I giving out of a sincere love, or is it perhaps pride or guilt?

Fourth, *deal with your own possessiveness* (v. 9). All of us are born with the stubborn tendency to hoard things for ourselves. Jesus, on the other hand, always sought to give.

Is a spirit of possessiveness keeping you from investing the riches God has given you in the lives of others?

It Costs Our Determined Commitment

A second cost connected with giving is commitment. The Corinthians' intention to give was a down payment of sorts; now Paul urges them to pay the price in full and complete their pledge.

I want to suggest that you finish what you started

35

to do a year ago, for you were not only the first to propose this idea, but the first to begin doing something about it. Having started the ball rolling so enthusiastically, you should carry this project through to completion just as gladly, giving whatever you can out of whatever you have. Let your enthusiastic idea at the start be equalled by your realistic action now. (vv. 10–11 LB)

A whole year had passed since the Corinthians' desire to give had first been sparked. During that time, however, their enthusiasm had sputtered and fizzled until nothing remained but the cold embers of a forgotten idea. So Paul encourages them to rekindle that intention and keep it lit with the fuel of a firm commitment.

Excitement and enthusiasm are great, but they rarely stick around for more than the grand opening of an idea. In between that and the finish line, during the long hours it takes to follow through on what we begin, commitment is our only companion and our encouragement to keep going. The Corinthians failed to give, not because they were short on money, but because they were short on commitment. That was the one cost they hadn't counted.

It Costs Our Exercising a Bold Faith

The final cost we'll consider is found in chapter 9, verses 6–8.

Now this I say, he who sows sparingly shall also reap sparingly; and he who sows bountifully shall also reap bountifully. Let each one do just as he has purposed in his heart; not grudgingly or under compulsion; for God loves a cheerful giver. And God is able to make all grace abound to you, that always having all sufficiency in everything, you may have an abundance for every good deed.

The guideline for giving is not presented as one arbitrary lump sum that everyone must fork over; rather, we're given a simple farming principle so that each of us can figure our own amounts. If we give sparingly, we will also reap sparingly. If, however, we exercise a bold faith like Christ's and give bountifully, we can expect a rich harvest. Now that doesn't mean we'll receive $200 for every $100 we give. "The rewards that the New Testament envisages are never material," writes William Barclay,

It promises not the wealth of things, but the wealth of the heart and of the spirit. What then can a generous man expect?

He will be *rich in love*. . . . Men will always prefer the warm heart, even though its very warmth may lead it into excesses, to the cold rectitude of the calculating spirit.

He will be *rich in friends*. . . . An unlovable man can never expect to be loved. The man whose heart runs out to others will always find that the hearts of others run out to him.

He will be *rich in help*. The day always comes when we need the help which others can give, and, if we have been sparing in our help to them, the likelihood is that they will be sparing in their help to us. The measure we have used to others will determine the measure which is given to us.

He will be *rich towards God*. Jesus taught us that what we do to others we do for God, and the day will come when every time we opened our heart and hand will stand to our favour, and every time we closed them will be a witness against us.[1]

Is It Worth It After All?

Even from Barclay's short list, it is clear that the rewards of giving far outweigh the costs. So don't give up on giving. Keep asking yourself the hard questions, examine your motives, pay the price of commitment, and exercise a bold faith. As soon as you get more, give more. As soon as you are blessed, share the blessing. And never overlook even the smallest opportunities to give, for in them you may find your greatest reward.

It is said that at the close of World War II, in war-ravaged London, a soldier happened to notice a young orphan with his face pressed against a warm bakery window. He followed the boy's eyes inside, where soft, steaming pastries were being taken out of the oven, the sweet aroma curling through the chill morning air. A slight moan brought his attention back to the boy, who was slowly

---

1. William Barclay, *The Letters to the Corinthians*, rev. ed., The Daily Study Bible Series (Philadelphia, Pa.: Westminster Press, 1975), pp. 234–35.

licking his hungry lips. The soldier's heart went out to him.

"Want some?" he asked the startled boy.

"Oh, yes sir . . . please."

As the soldier opened the door, a gush of fragrant warmth enveloped the boy. A few minutes later, the soldier smiled and handed him a bagful of piping-hot pastries. As he turned to walk away, he felt a slight tug at his sleeve.

"Mister," the boy asked softly, "are you God?"

Truly, we are never more like God than when we give.[2]

Living Insights   STUDY ONE

Can you believe those Corinthians? Hypocrites, all of them. "Count us in!" they said with cloying sincerity. "We want to give, we care about our brothers and sisters in Jerusalem!" Talk, talk, talk. For a whole year all they did was talk about what they were going to do—without ever getting it done. Can you believe that? You can bet I've never . . .

well, almost never . . .

what I mean is . . .

I, uh, at least not in the last six months have I ever . . .

OK, OK, I admit it. I've done the very same thing. Haven't we all, really? How many times, even in the last year, have we intended to give or talked about giving or prayed about giving without ever following through?

Perhaps there's something nagging at your conscience right now. Did you promise to do something for someone three weeks ago and it still isn't done? Have you pledged to support your church or a ministry or an individual and, months later, still aren't giving anything? Has the Spirit of God impressed upon you to give of your time and talents to meet a need, and you're still putting it off?

If there is something that comes to mind, let Paul's words be a personal reminder to you.

> But now finish doing it also; that just as there was
> the readiness to desire it, so there may be also the
> completion of it by your ability. (2 Cor. 8:11)

2. Adapted from *Illustrations Unlimited*, ed. James S. Hewett (Wheaton, Ill.: Tyndale House Publishers, 1988), p. 304.

Use the space provided to write down the giving you need to follow through on and how you plan to do it—as soon as possible!

Area of giving: _____

Follow-through plan: _____

_____

_____

_____

🍵 *Living Insights* _____ STUDY TWO

When was the last time you conducted a thorough examination of your giving? For many of us, the embarrassing answer is never. That's not to say we don't give; it's just that we haven't ever sat down to carefully assess our giving as Paul challenged the Corinthians to do.

If that's you, perhaps it would help if you used the four practical insights from the lesson to strengthen your giving as a servant. Take your time with this, and allow the Spirit of God to work as you consider each issue.

- *Seek the objectivity of another person.* Is there someone you could ask to evaluate your giving, someone whose spiritual maturity in this area you respect?_____

  When?_____

  Record here a brief description of the things you want to discuss.

  _____

  _____

  _____

- *Ask hard questions of yourself.* For the Corinthians, that meant dealing with the probing question, Why are you so strong in faith, teaching, knowledge, and love, but not in giving? Today, would this same question apply to you? If so, why?

  _____

  _____

- *Examine your motives.* Are you motivated to give by a love for others that comes in response to Jesus' love for you? Or is pride pushing you on? Is it guilt? Do you give grudgingly or cheerfully?

- *Deal with your own possessiveness.* How often do you notice your knuckles whitening around what is yours? What mental process do you go through to relax your grip and open your hands?

Chapter 6

THE SERVANT AS A FORGIVER

(PART ONE)

2 Corinthians 2:4–11; Matthew 5:23–24

Forgiveness . . . it is a sacred act, a priestly service. It is tears of deepest sorrow and joyous relief. It is humiliation and affirmation. It is guilt grappling with grace, pain pursuing peace. It is, however we describe it, one of the most powerful acts of servanthood we can participate in—and one of the most difficult. Consider, for example, Simon Wiesenthal's haunting experience while imprisoned in a German concentration camp.

> He was selected at random from a work detail, yanked aside, and taken up a back stairway to a hospital corridor. A nurse led him into a darkened room, then left him alone with a pitiful figure wrapped in white, lying on a bed. It was a German officer, badly wounded, swathed in yellow-stained bandages. Gauze covered his entire face.
>
> In a weakened, trembling voice, the officer proceeded to offer a kind of sacramental confession to Wiesenthal. He recounted his boyhood and early days in the Hitler Youth movement. He told of action along the Russian front, and of the increasingly harsh measures his SS unit had taken against the Jewish populace. And then he told of a terrible atrocity, when his unit herded all the Jews from one town into a wooden frame building and torched it. Some of the Jews, their clothes and hair ablaze, leaped in desperation from the second floor, and the SS soldiers—he among them—shot them as they fell. He started to tell of one child in particular, a young boy with black hair and dark eyes, but his voice gave way.
>
> Several times Wiesenthal tried to leave the room, but each time the mummy-like figure would reach out with a cold, bloodless hand and constrain him.

41

Finally, after maybe two hours, the officer explained why he had summoned a Jewish prisoner. He had asked a nurse whether any Jews still existed; if so, he wanted one brought to his room for a last rite before death. "I know that what I am asking is almost too much for you," he said. "But without your answer I cannot die in peace." And then he asked for forgiveness for all his crimes against the Jews. He was imploring a prisoner who the next day might die at the hands of SS comrades.

Wiesenthal stood in silence for some time, staring at the man's bandaged face. At last he made up his mind and left the room, without saying a word. He left the soldier in torment, unforgiven.[1]

None of us, thank God, will probably ever have to deal with forgiveness in such chilling circumstances. Nevertheless, we will struggle, we will agonize, we will grope to administer this incredible sacrament of servanthood.

A First-Century Account of Forgiveness

To find out more about our servant's role as forgiver, let's examine an incident involving the early church at Corinth, where another sinner was left in torment, unforgiven.

Background

Our first glimpse into this particular situation comes through a stinging rebuke written by the apostle Paul in his first letter to the Corinthians.

It is actually reported that there is immorality among you, and immorality of such a kind as does not exist even among the Gentiles, that someone has his father's wife. And you have become arrogant, and have not mourned instead, in order that the one who had done this deed might be removed from your midst. For I, on my part, though absent in body but present in spirit, have already judged him who has

1. Philip Yancey, *I Was Just Wondering* (Grand Rapids, Mich.: William B. Eerdmans Publishing Co., 1989), pp. 70–73.

so committed this, as though I were present. In the name of our Lord Jesus, when you are assembled, and I with you in spirit, with the power of our Lord Jesus, I have decided to deliver such a one to Satan for the destruction of his flesh, that his spirit may be saved in the day of the Lord Jesus. (5:1–5)

A member of the church openly commits incest, and they're not doing anything about it? Paul is incredulous. How can this be? Worse still, how can the Corinthians apparently boast about their broad-minded acceptance of this Christian's immoral behavior? The man needs correction, not coddling, Paul tells them. And so he earnestly enjoins the Corinthians to remove the wicked man from their midst, to disassociate themselves from him, to refuse him any fellowship (vv. 11, 13).

Why? So "that his spirit may be saved" (v. 5). The purpose of discipline is restoration, not simply retribution. And the Apostle also mentions his concern for the church's purity. The leaven of this man's sin has contaminated the Corinthians' character and witness, which also needs to be restored by his removal (vv. 6–8).[2]

Call to Forgive

Eager to obey Paul's advice, the Corinthians zealously discipline the man guilty of incest. So much so that even after he confesses and repents of his sin, they still deny him fellowship in the church. Six to twelve months pass and this is still going on when the Apostle pens his second letter to the Corinthians. In this epistle he calls for their correction to cease. The discipline has accomplished its purpose, and now it is time to offer forgiveness and complete this believer's restoration to the body.

> Sufficient for such a one is this punishment which was inflicted by the majority, so that on the contrary you should rather forgive and comfort him, lest somehow such a one be overwhelmed by excessive sorrow. Wherefore I urge you to reaffirm your love for him. For to this end also I wrote that I might put you to the test, whether you are obedient in all

---

2. That Paul says nothing about disciplining the stepmother in this case seems to indicate that she wasn't a believer.

things. But whom you forgive anything, I forgive also; for indeed what I have forgiven, if I have forgiven anything, I did it for your sakes in the presence of Christ, in order that no advantage be taken of us by Satan; for we are not ignorant of his schemes. (2:6–11)

Forgive, comfort, reaffirm your love—in beautiful balance, Paul exhorts the Corinthians to welcome back this repentant sinner with the same zealous intensity that characterized their enforcement of his discipline. He wants them to quickly run and embrace this prodigal. Welcome him back home. Let forgiveness work its cleansing effect on this man's conscience, let it bring healing where there has only been hurt, let it restore unity where there has only been division. Kill the fatted calf and celebrate!

The importance of this forgiveness is underscored by Paul's caution in verse 11. Had the Corinthians continued withholding forgiveness from this man, ignoring his repentant attitude, Satan would have gained all the advantage he needed to cause him to despair.

Need to Repent

Later on in this same letter, Paul delineates the power of a repentant spirit.

For the sorrow that is according to the will of God produces a repentance without regret, leading to salvation; but the sorrow of the world produces death. (7:10)

This godly sorrow Paul focuses on is initiated by a humble and contrite heart, a heart open to the truth. This sorrow then produces change, a turning away from sin that is, in essence, what repentance means. This truth-driven change, in turn, leads the way to life-giving choices, since the truth is a "lamp unto [our] feet" that lights our way along the path of life (Ps. 119:105). In summary, we could say that an open, receptive, vulnerable heart releases the power of God's truth because it invites Him in and makes a place for His presence in our lives.

The sorrow of the world, on the contrary, is not a sorrow that produces a desire to change. The only desire it generates is an urge to get rid of the painful consequences of sin, rather than a commitment to deal with the sinful choices that caused the pain in the first place. The heart of worldly sorrow is proud—too proud to admit the need of a Savior; and it is closed—shut off to receiving the truth that would turn it toward life. So it traps itself in the unending ache of irredeemable regret, forever condemning itself to constant grief and hopelessness (2 Cor. 7:10b).

The truth of this verse can shed much light on Paul's plea for the Corinthians to forgive and restore their repentant brother. This man had come through sorrow, had opened himself to the truth and changed his course, and was now ready to reenter the freedom and acceptance that Christ offers us all. But the Corinthians, in their earnest zeal to do right, were unwittingly blocking him from the path of life. They were prolonging his sorrow, his ache; what they needed to do was affirm his changed heart and their acceptance of him. This would be accomplished if they reached out to meet him in forgiveness.

And perhaps they, too, needed to repent—needed to confess a harsh, closed spirit of their own. For it takes two softened hearts to build the bridge of restored relationship (compare Col. 3:12–13 with 2 Cor. 5:18).

Our Forgiveness of One Another

If we look closely, we can see that there are basically two roles in the forgiveness process: the role of the offender and of the offended. For the remainder of this chapter, we will focus on how a servant should respond when he or she is the offender.

When We Are the Offender

In a nutshell, Matthew 5:23–24 describes the correct procedure to follow when we have offended someone.

> "If therefore you are presenting your offering at the altar, and there remember that your brother has something against you, leave your offering there before the altar, and go your way; first be reconciled to your brother, and then come and present your offering."

The scene depicted in verse 23 is that of a worshiper in Jesus' day bringing animals or birds to be sacrificed for the forgiveness of sins. Imagine for a moment that this worshiper is you. You're at the altar, on your knees, perhaps, when suddenly your conscience is pricked by the fact that you have offended someone. What do you do? Verse 24 outlines four steps:

1. Stop—"leave your offering there"
2. Go—"go your way"
3. Reconcile—"first be reconciled"
4. Return—"then come and present your offering"

The key term is *reconciled.* It comes from a Greek verb meaning "to alter, to change," with a prefix added that means "through." Combined, they communicate the idea that we're to go through a process that will result in change. In other words, as the offender, we are to go and confess the wrong to the offended and seek forgiveness—ideally, in person; if that's not possible, however, at least by phone or letter. *Then* we are free to return and worship God.

As simple as this process sounds, it is not always easy. Internal doubts and apprehensions can assail our minds and prevent us from carrying this process out. To circumvent the paralyzing power of these doubts, let's face several common "what if" situations head-on.

1. *What if he or she refuses to forgive?*
   The important thing for each of us to remember is that you are responsible for *you* and I am responsible for *me*. With the right motive, in the right spirit, at the right time, out of obedience to God, we are to humble ourselves (remember, it is servanthood we're developing) and attempt to make things right. God will honor our efforts. The one offended may need time—first to get over the shock and next, to have God bring about a change in his or her heart. Healing sometimes takes time. Occasionally, a lot of time.[3]

2. *What if the situation only gets worse?*
   This can happen. You see, all the time the one offended has been blaming you . . . mentally sticking pins in your doll . . . thinking all kinds of bad things about you. When you go to make things right, you suddenly cause his internal scales to go out of balance. You take away the blame and all that's left

---

3. Charles R. Swindoll, *Improving Your Serve: The Art of Unselfish Living* (Waco, Tex.: Word Books Publisher, 1981), p. 60.

is the person's guilt, which does a number on him, resulting in even worse feelings.[4]

3. *What if I decide to simply deal with it before God and not go through the hassle and embarrassment of talking with the other person?*
We'll do *anything* to make things easier, won't we? Well, first off—that is a willful contradiction of the command. Jesus says, "Stop, go, reconcile, and return!" *Not* to go is direct disobedience. It also can result in things getting worse.

Let's say I am driving away from your church parking lot next Sunday morning. I back my car into the side of your beautiful, new *Mercedes*. . . . CRUNCH! You are visiting with friends following the service and you hear the noise. Your stomach churns as you see me get out of the car, look at the damage . . . and then bow in prayer:

Dear Lord, please forgive me for being so preoccupied and clumsy. And please give John grace as he sees the extensive damage I have caused out of sheer negligence. And provide his needs as he takes this car in to have it fixed. Thanks, Lord. Amen.

As I drive away, I wave and smile real big as I yell out the window, "It's all cleared up, John. I claimed the damage before God. *Isn't grace wonderful!*"

Tell me, how does that grab you? I have rather strong doubts that it would suddenly make things A-O.K., no matter how sincere my prayer might have been. You and I know that would do no good.

. . . Wounded souls are offended people. And the Savior does not say, "Simply pray and I'll forgive you." In fact, He says, "Stop praying until you have made things right!" That is the part of the "forgiveness exam" that's tough to pass.[5]

4. *What if it is impossible for me to seek reconciliation because the offended person has died?*

4. Swindoll, *Improving Your Serve*, pp. 60–61.

5. Swindoll, *Improving Your Serve*, p. 61.

In such unique cases, I recommend that you share your burden of guilt with someone whom you can trust. A close friend, your mate, a counselor, or your pastor. Be specific and completely candid. Pray with that individual and confess openly the wrong and the guilt of your soul. In such cases—and only in such cases—prayer and the presence of an understanding, affirming individual will provide the relief you need so desperately.[6]

Now that we've examined the procedure the offender should follow, we'll turn our attention in the next chapter to the flip side of forgiveness and consider the servant's role when offended.

📖 *Living Insights* STUDY ONE

"If therefore you are presenting your offering at the altar, and there remember that your brother has something against you, leave your offering there before the altar, and go your way; first be reconciled to your brother, and then come and present your offering." (Matt. 5:23–24)

Only two verses. We read them so quickly, so, so . . . what's the word—*familiarly*—that this brief vignette from the Sermon on the Mount hardly raises a ripple in many of our minds. "Yes, yes, altars and offerings, isn't that nice." And we skip across to the next passage without really seeing or hearing it.

And yet there is nothing shallow about Jesus' words. Nothing superficial about His concern. And certainly nothing simple about His challenge. Walk with Him here, in the humbling truth of these two verses, and your attitude, your relationship with others, your whole life will be different.

Are we serious about servanthood? Then perhaps we should go back, with William Barclay's help, and look more carefully at what Jesus is saying to us, to me, to you.

The picture which Jesus is painting is very vivid. The worshipper, of course, did not make his own

6. Swindoll, *Improving Your Serve*, p. 62.

sacrifice; he brought it to the priest who offered it on his behalf. The worshipper has entered the Temple; he has passed through its series of courts, the Court of the Gentiles, the Court of the Women, the Court of the Men. Beyond that there lay the Court of the Priests into which the layman could not go. The worshipper is standing at the rail, ready to hand over his victim to the priest; his hands are on it to confess; and then he remembers his breach with his brother, the wrong done to his brother; if his sacrifice is to avail, he must go back and mend that breach and undo that wrong, or nothing can happen. . . .

. . . The breach between man and God could not be healed until the breach between man and man was healed. If a man was making a sin-offering, for instance, to atone for a theft, the offering was held to be completely unavailing until the thing stolen had been restored; and, if it was discovered that the thing had not been restored, then the sacrifice had to be destroyed as unclean and burned outside the Temple. . . .

Jesus is quite clear about this basic fact—we cannot be right with God until we are right with men; we cannot hope for forgiveness until we have confessed our sin, not only to God, but also to men, and until we have done our best to remove the practical consequences of it. We sometimes wonder why there is a barrier between us and God; we sometimes wonder why our prayers seem unavailing. The reason may well be that we ourselves have erected that barrier, through being at variance with our fellow-men, or because we have wronged someone and have done nothing to put things right.[7]

Is there someone you've wronged with whom you need to be reconciled?

Who?_____

7. William Barclay, *The Gospel of Matthew*, vol. 1, rev. ed., The Daily Study Bible Series (Philadelphia, Pa.: Westminster Press, 1975), pp. 142–43. Used by kind permission of The Saint Andrew Press, Edinburgh, Scotland.

What needs confessing? If you're hesitant about answering, consider these direct, yet reassuring, words from Psalm 51.

> For Thou dost not delight in sacrifice, otherwise I
>   would give it;
> Thou art not pleased with burnt offering.
> The sacrifices of God are a broken spirit;
> A broken and a contrite heart, O God, Thou wilt
>   not despise.
> (vv. 16–17)

_____

_____

_____

What practical consequences can you remove in this situation?

_____

_____

_____

The prophet Samuel once wrote,

> "Has the Lord as much delight in burnt offerings
>   and sacrifices
> As in obeying the voice of the Lord?
> Behold, to obey is better than sacrifice,
> And to heed than the fat of rams."
> (1 Sam. 15:22)

Go now, and obey Jesus' voice to reconcile yourself with this other person.

📖 Living Insights

How did it go with that person you wronged?
"Uh, well, I . . ."
You didn't go and reconcile, did you?
"Not yet."
Not yet? When?

Chapter 7

THE SERVANT AS A FORGIVER
(PART TWO)
Matthew 18:21–35

From the crest of the hill we saw it, like a vast scar
on the green German landscape; a city of low gray
barracks surrounded by concrete walls on which
guard towers rose at intervals. In the very center, a
square smokestack emitted a thin gray vapor into
the blue sky.

"Ravensbruck!"

Like a whispered curse the word passed back
through the lines. This was the notorious women's
extermination camp whose name we had heard even
in Haarlem. That squat concrete building, that smoke
disappearing in the bright sunlight—no! I would
not look at it![1]

For many, hell is just a myth, a make-believe place of misery and
torment reserved for the damned. But for prisoners like Corrie
ten Boom and her sister Betsie, whom the Nazis condemned for
helping Jews escape through the Dutch underground, there was
nothing mythical about it. Hell was real; they had just arrived.

It was the third night as we were getting ready
to lie down again under the sky when the order came
to report to the processing center for new arrivals.
A ten-minute march brought us to the building. We
inched along a corridor into a huge reception room.
And there under the harsh ceiling lights we saw a
dismal sight. As each woman reached a desk where
some officers sat she had to lay her blanket, pillow-
case, and whatever else she carried onto a growing
pile of these things. A few desks further along she

---

1. Corrie ten Boom, with John and Elizabeth Sherrill, *The Hiding Place* (New York, N.Y.:
Bantam Books, 1971), p. 189. Used by permission of Chosen Books.

51

had to strip off every scrap of clothes, throw them onto a second pile, and walk naked past the scrutiny of a dozen S.S. men into the shower room. Coming out of the shower she wore only a thin prison dress and a pair of shoes. Nothing more.[2]

Corrie ten Boom never forgot that night or the nightmare that followed. Altogether, ninety-six thousand women died at Ravens-bruck, one of whom was Betsie. Just two days after her sister's death, Corrie was miraculously released and returned home.[3]

In the years immediately following, Corrie carried the healing message of the gospel throughout Europe, encouraging people to replace the bitterness and hate of war with God's forgiveness and love. Nowhere was this message needed more desperately than in Germany. It was while speaking there that Corrie's faith in her own message was unexpectedly put to the test.

It was at a church service in Munich that I saw him, the former S.S. man who had stood guard at the shower room door in the processing center at Ravensbruck. He was the first of our actual jailers that I had seen since that time. And suddenly it was all there—the roomful of mocking men, the heaps of clothing, Betsie's pain-blanched face.

He came up to me as the church was emptying, beaming and bowing. "How grateful I am for your message, *Fraulein*," he said. "To think that, as you say, He has washed my sins away!"

His hand was thrust out to shake mine. And I, who had preached so often to the people in Bloemendaal the need to forgive, kept my hand at my side.

Even as the angry, vengeful thoughts boiled through me, I saw the sin of them. Jesus Christ had died for this man; was I going to ask for more? Lord Jesus, I prayed, forgive me and help me to forgive him.

I tried to smile, I struggled to raise my hand. I could not. I felt nothing, not the slightest spark of

2. Ten Boom, *The Hiding Place*, p. 191.

3. In 1959 Corrie revisited Ravensbruck and learned that her release had been the result of a clerical error. One week later all women her age had been sent to the gas chambers (*The Hiding Place*, p. 241).

warmth or charity. And so again I breathed a silent prayer. Jesus, I cannot forgive him. Give me Your forgiveness.

As I took his hand the most incredible thing happened. From my shoulder along my arm and through my hand a current seemed to pass from me to him, while into my heart sprang a love for this stranger that almost overwhelmed me.

And so I discovered that it is not on our forgiveness any more than on our goodness that the world's healing hinges, but on His. When He tells us to love our enemies, He gives, along with the command, the love itself.[4]

Two Servants, Same Need

Corrie ten Boom's act of forgiveness is utterly amazing. That she would bestow such an astonishing gift of grace upon her former captor and tormentor is nothing short of miraculous. And all the more so when you consider that she was not an "exceptional person, but, in her own words, 'a very weak and ordinary one.'"[5]

The truth is, we're all weak and ordinary, especially when we've been hurt by someone else. For it's at that very moment when forgiveness is desperately needed that we feel too weak to give it, and our ordinariness quickly surfaces in feelings of hate and revenge. Isn't that how Corrie felt? Yet she was able to go on and perform one of life's greatest miracles. How could she? And how can we?

Let's find out by listening to Corrie's Master, as He teaches in Matthew 18.

Question and Answer

Peter, probably the most outspoken of the disciples, has just approached Jesus with a question concerning the limits of forgiveness.

> "Lord, how often shall my brother sin against me and I forgive him? Up to seven times?" (v. 21)

Peter must have thought he was putting forth a magnanimous

4. Ten Boom, *The Hiding Place*, p. 238.
5. Ten Boom, *The Hiding Place*, p. 242.

offer, because the rabbis in that day said to forgive only three times. Imagine his shock, then, at Jesus' answer.

> "I do not say to you, up to seven times, but up to seventy times seven." (v. 22)

Playing off Peter's number, Christ comes up with a figure that was obviously not meant to be taken literally. Rather, it was intended to convey to his fisherman follower and the rest of the disciples that their forgiveness of one another should have no limits.

No limits? "Now wait a minute," the disciples must have thought. This was too much for them to fathom. And it must have been obvious by the frowns on their faces and their furtive glances of disbelief. So Jesus expands their limited thinking with a parable.

Parable and Analogy

As we look closely at Jesus' story, we'll find that He sets forth two dimensions of forgiveness. The first, in verses 23–27, is the *vertical*: God's forgiveness of sinners.

> "For this reason the kingdom of heaven may be compared to a certain king who wished to settle accounts with his slaves. And when he had begun to settle them, there was brought to him one who owed him ten thousand talents. But since he did not have the means to repay, his lord commanded him to be sold, along with his wife and children and all that he had, and repayment to be made. The slave therefore falling down, prostrated himself before him, saying, 'Have patience with me, and I will repay you everything.' And the lord of that slave felt compassion and released him and forgave him the debt."

You can hardly appreciate the debt that's been forgiven without first understanding the amount of money owed. One talent in that day was probably a measure of gold somewhere between fifty and eighty pounds.[6] Multiply that by ten thousand and you can see just how gracious the king's forgiveness really was.

---

6. This "servant owed a large amount, 10,000 talents. This probably equaled several million dollars." Louis A. Barbieri, Jr., "Matthew," in *The Bible Knowledge Commentary*, New Testament ed. (Wheaton, Ill.: Scripture Press Publications, Victor Books, 1983), p. 62.

Notice also how the last line sums up the salient points about vertical forgiveness: compassion of the king, release from wrong, and forgiveness of the sinner.

What a perfect analogy between Almighty God and sinful humanity! Moved by compassion and love . . . the Father sent His Son to release us from sin . . . by canceling out our debt through His death—total forgiveness. Perhaps it was this very parable the apostle Paul had in mind when he later wrote:

> And when you were dead in your transgressions and the uncircumcision of your flesh, He made you alive together with Him, having forgiven us all our transgressions, having canceled out the certificate of debt consisting of decrees against us and which was hostile to us; and He has taken it out of the way, having nailed it to the cross. (Col. 2:13–14)

Because of our sin, each of us has owed God a debt we could not pay. Yet He graciously paid it for us with the life and blood of His own Son. Until we grasp that, until we see the infinite depth of His forgiveness in light of our own sinfulness, none of us will be prepared to deal with the second dimension of Jesus' parable, which focuses on the *horizontal*: our forgiveness of one another.

> "But that slave went out and found one of his fellow slaves who owed him a hundred denarii;[7] and he seized him and began to choke him, saying, 'Pay back what you owe.' So his fellow slave fell down and began to entreat him, saying, 'Have patience with me and I will repay you.' He was unwilling however, but went and threw him in prison until he should pay back what was owed. So when his fellow slaves saw what had happened, they were deeply grieved and came and reported to their lord all that had happened. Then summoning him, his lord said

---

7. "Though drawn in British currency, this contrast pictured by A. R. S. Kennedy between the two debts is unmistakably clear: Suppose they were paid in sixpences [coins equivalent to six U.S. pennies]. The 100 denarii debt could be carried in one pocket. The ten thousand talent debt would take to carry it an army of about 8,600 carriers, each carrying a sack of sixpences 60 lbs. in weight; and they would form, at a distance of a yard apart, a line five miles long!" As quoted by William Barclay in *The Gospel of Matthew*, vol. 2, rev. ed., The Daily Study Bible Series (Philadelphia, Pa.: Westminster Press, 1975), p. 194.

to him, 'You wicked slave, I forgave you all that debt because you entreated me. Should you not also have had mercy on your fellow slave, even as I had mercy on you?' And his lord, moved with anger, handed him over to the torturers until he should repay all that was owed him. So shall My heavenly Father also do to you, if each of you does not forgive his brother from your heart." (Matt. 18:28–35)

"There are two reasons," Ray Stedman noted from this passage, "why Christians must forgive each other."

First, we must forgive because anything less is hypocritical. We cannot demand justice from others because we do not stand on that ground ourselves. . . . This is what Jesus is saying to us. We must forgive one another because we have already been forgiven. Is not that the ground the apostle Paul takes in Colossians 3, and in Ephesians 4:31?

Let all bitterness and wrath and anger and clamor and slander be put away from you, with all malice, and be kind to one another, tender-hearted, *forgiving one another, as God in Christ forgave you.*

That is the basis of Christian forgiveness. Jesus says that when we refuse to do this, when we hold a grudge, or are difficult or bitter and refuse to settle an issue, then we are doing exactly what this unrighteous steward does here. . . .

The second reason we must forgive is because of the torment which an unforgiving spirit inflicts upon us. . . .

["Delivered to the torturers"] is a marvelously expressive phrase to describe what happens to us when we do not forgive another. It is an accurate description of gnawing resentment and bitterness, the awful gall of hate or envy. It is a terrible feeling. We cannot get away from it, we cannot escape it. We find ourselves powerless to avoid it. We feel strongly this separation from another and every time we think of them we feel within the acid of resentment and hate eating away at our peace and calmness. This is the torturing that our Lord says will take place.[8]

Two Solutions, Same Issue

The next time you find yourself confronted with the need to forgive someone who has hurt you, remember to *focus first and fully on God's forgiveness of you.* Allow yourself plenty of time to think through how infinite God's mercy has been toward you. Recall some of the specific wrongs you've committed; consider His grace in canceling those debts; bless the Lord, as David did, for removing your sin as far as the east is from the west (see Ps. 103).

The measure to which you can envision God's forgiveness of you will be the same measure by which you are able to forgive others.

Also remember to *deal directly and honestly with any resentment you harbor against others.* Are you holding a grudge against someone in your family, a brother or sister, son or father-in-law? Could it be a friend, a boss, perhaps another Christian, or an individual you dated? Should you not also have mercy on this person even as Jesus has had mercy on you?

🍺 *Living Insights* STUDY ONE

In his book *When You Can't Come Back,* Dave Dravecky writes:

> From spending so much time in hospitals, I've learned that when we walk through someone's door who is suffering, we have to respect the sanctity of that room. When we cross that threshold, we should be careful not to violate that person's life. Something sacred happens when a person is suffering. There is a turning to God, turning to him for assurance, for answers, for comfort.[9]

Even now, many of you are suffering from what someone has done to you. Perhaps it was a close friend's betrayal, a trusted leader's

---

8. Ray Stedman, "Breaking the Resentment Barrier," Treasures of the Parables series (Palo Alto, Calif.: Discovery Publishing, n.d.), pp. 2–3.

9. Dave and Jan Dravecky, with Ken Gire, *When You Can't Come Back* (Grand Rapids, Mich.: Zondervan Publishing House, HarperSanFrancisco, 1992), p. 70.

lies, or a spouse's abandonment. Your bitterness and anger are intense. For me to enter into your need to forgive that person is to walk through a personal door of suffering. Be assured, I have no desire to barge into the privacy of that pain and trespass all over your feelings. Nor do I want to trivialize your struggle by patting you on the arm and reciting a few preachy platitudes that are supposed to fix everything.

And least of all do I want to leave you feeling violated a second time by presuming to tell you that you must forgive this person. I have no right to demand such an extraordinary thing. I don't even know you. Neither have I experienced any of your suffering. Only one other Person has, and He alone has the right to come knocking at your door asking you to forgive. That Person is Jesus.

He knows the pain of rejection, the violence of abuse, the unfairness of being misunderstood and maligned. Greatest of all, He knows the unfairness of having to suffer and die for sins He did not commit. My sins. Your sins.

Will you open the door to begin looking at ways the forgiveness Christ has given you can be extended to others? Perhaps joining the psalmist in praising God for His complete forgiveness in Psalm 103 would be a good place to start.

▌🍵 *Living Insights* STUDY TWO

Many of us fumble with forgiveness simply because we hate confrontation—we're willing to do just about anything to avoid it. But, as Lewis Smedes points out in *Forgive and Forget*, true forgiveness is possible only when we have the toughness to face reality.

> To be able to forgive we must have the guts to look hard at the wrongness, the horridness, the sheer wickedness of what somebody did to us. We cannot camouflage; we cannot excuse; we cannot ignore. We eye the evil face to face and we call it what it is. Only realists can be forgivers.
>
> One prime reason why some people cannot forgive is their fear of reality. Parents miss chances to forgive their children because they are afraid to face the facts. A mother has a sixth sense that her son

is stealing money from her. He needs money to buy drugs for himself and gas for his van; but he has lost his job. So he pilfers at home. She misses a ten-dollar bill here, a twenty there, out of her purse and out of her dresser drawer. He leaves hints behind, clear enough to give himself away. She knows; but she refuses to acknowledge what she knows. She stuffs her knowledge safely into her subconscious bag of unpleasant facts. She closes her eyes and she avoids the crisis of forgiving.

Self-deception is a lot easier than forgiving. But it has no payoff in healing.

Forgiving begins with the power to shake off deception and deal with reality.[10]

Are you one of those who pretends to turn the other cheek to avoid confronting sin and offering forgiveness?

Whose help could you seek to shake off this pattern of deception and learn how to deal with reality? _____

What personal experience of ignoring sin and avoiding forgiveness could you talk about with this person?

_____

_____

_____

Will you share this with the person you named? Or are you already talking yourself out of confronting this sin?

10. Lewis B. Smedes, *Forgive and Forget: Healing the Hurts We Don't Deserve* (New York, N.Y.: Simon and Schuster, Pocket Books, 1984), pp. 179–80.

Chapter 8

THE SERVANT AS A FORGETTER

Philippians 3:7–14

Among the greatest of God's creations is the human mind. And perhaps the most astounding part of that creation is the internal filing system wedged within its creases known as memory. In his book *You and Your Thoughts*, Earl D. Radmacher shows just how astounding it is.

> The human mind is a fabulous computer. As a matter of fact, no one has been able to design a computer as intricate and efficient as the human mind. Consider this: your brain is capable of recording 800 memories per second for seventy-five years without ever getting tired. Although there are a number of computers on the market today with amazing capabilities packed into them, not one of them can match the service record of the human brain. . . .
>
> I have heard some persons complain that their brain is too tired to get involved in a program of Scripture memorization. I have news for them—the body can get tired, but the brain never does. A human being doesn't use more than 2 percent of his brain power, scientists tell us. And, of course, some demonstrate this fact more obviously than others. The point is, the brain is capable of an incredible amount of work and it retains everything it takes in. You never really forget anything; you just don't recall it. Everything is on permanent file in your brain.[1]

If everything is permanently filed inside our brains—including all the offenses we've suffered—then how can we forget a wrong done against us? Is it even possible? For help in answering these questions, let's turn to four passages of Scripture. The first three

---

1. Earl D. Radmacher, *You and Your Thoughts: The Power of Right Thinking* (Wheaton, Ill.: Tyndale House, 1977), pp. 15, 19.

we'll look at briefly, like a rock skipping across a lake. Then we'll settle on the fourth, found in Philippians 3, and examine it more deeply.

An Overview of Forgetting

To begin, we should clarify the meaning of *forgetting* as it will be used in this chapter. We don't mean to forget in the literal, technical sense of the word, but in the spiritual sense reflected in 1 Corinthians 13:4–5.

> Love is patient, love is kind, and is not jealous; love does not brag and is not arrogant, does not act unbecomingly; it does not seek its own, is not provoked, *does not take into account a wrong suffered.* (emphasis added)

J. B. Phillips' translation renders the last part of verse 5 this way: "It does not keep account of evil." Or, as *Webster's* puts it, to forget is "to treat with inattention or disregard . . . overlook."[2] In other words servants who are motivated by God's love don't keep meticulous mental ledgers of all the wrongs that have ever been committed against them.

But that's not all. We can expand this definition and our understanding still further with two more passages that encourage this servant's attitude. First, Psalm 119:165:

> Those who love Thy law have great peace,
> And nothing causes them to stumble.

In his book *Improving Your Serve*, Chuck Swindoll interprets this verse as follows:

> The psalmist openly declares that those who possess a deep love for God's Word will have great measures of His *shalom* . . . and, in addition, they will be big enough to resist stumbling over offenses.[3]

Our definition gains more clarity and shape when we link this thought with Jesus' words against a judgmental spirit.

---

2. *Webster's Ninth New Collegiate Dictionary*, see "forget."

3. Charles R. Swindoll, *Improving Your Serve: The Art of Unselfish Living* (Waco, Tex.: Word Books Publisher, 1981), p. 72.

"Do not judge lest you be judged. For in the way you judge, you will be judged; and by your standard of measure, it will be measured to you. And why do you look at the speck that is in your brother's eye, but do not notice the log that is in your own eye? Or how can you say to your brother, 'Let me take the speck out of your eye,' and behold, the log is in your own eye? You hypocrite, first take the log out of your own eye, and then you will see clearly to take the speck out of your brother's eye." (Matt. 7:1–5)

When you distill the truths from the three passages noted thus far, a composite picture develops that defines forgetting as

- Refusing to keep score,

- Being bigger than an offense, and

- Harboring no judgmental attitude.

Forgetting offenses is only half the picture, however. The other half, which we'll find in Paul's letter to the Philippians, defines forgetting as

the ability to go on beyond our own good deeds. Once they are done, they're done. No need to drop little hints on how thoughtful we were. Improving our serve includes forgetting our service.[4]

A Close Look at Forgetting

If anyone ever had reason to boast about his or her service record, it would be the apostle Paul. His reputation as a Law-abiding Pharisee was impeccable. And to prove it, he lists his credentials early on in chapter 3 of Philippians.

If anyone else has a mind to put confidence in the flesh, I far more: circumcised the eighth day, of the nation of Israel, of the tribe of Benjamin, a Hebrew of Hebrews; as to the Law, a Pharisee; as to zeal, a persecutor of the church; as to the righteousness which is in the Law, found blameless. (vv. 4b–6)

---

4. Swindoll, *Improving Your Serve*, p. 72.

Paul's achievements were impressive. However, instead of brag about them, he goes on to reflect on them from the perspective of a servant who's a forgetter.

> But whatever things were gain to me, those things I have counted as loss for the sake of Christ. More than that, I count all things to be loss in view of the surpassing value of knowing Christ Jesus my Lord, for whom I have suffered the loss of all things, and count them but rubbish in order that I may gain Christ, and may be found in Him, not having a righteousness of my own derived from the Law, but that which is through faith in Christ, the righteousness which comes from God on the basis of faith. (vv. 7–9)

What was it that enabled Paul to cultivate such an attitude? We get a glimpse, perhaps, a few lines later when he states:

> I don't mean to say I am perfect. I haven't learned all I should even yet, but I keep working toward that day when I will finally be all that Christ saved me for and wants me to be.
>
> No, dear brothers, I am still not all I should be but I am bringing all my energies to bear on this one thing: Forgetting the past and looking forward to what lies ahead, I strain to reach the end of the race and receive the prize for which God is calling us up to heaven because of what Christ Jesus did for us. (vv. 12–14 LB)

Tucked away in these verses are three thoughts that help clarify what it means to forget like a servant:

- I have not arrived

- I forget what is behind

- I move on to what is ahead

Let's take a close look at these statements and their respective issues of vulnerability, humility, and determination.

Vulnerability

"I have not arrived." Three times in verses 12–13a the Apostle openly admits to being human and flawed: first, "Not that I have already obtained it" (v. 12a); second, "or have already become perfect" (v. 12b); and third, "I do not regard myself as having laid hold of it yet" (v. 13a).

Here's a brilliant and gifted leader who freely declares, "I don't have everything wired." How refreshing! And how rare. Those who lack such vulnerability tend to have greater difficulty forgetting the wrongs of others than those who are willing to admit personal needs, confess limitations and failures, and have a teachable spirit.

In his book *The Velvet Covered Brick*, author Howard Butt writes with pointed practicality about the importance of being vulnerable.

> If your leadership is Christian you can openly reveal your failures. Leaders who are fully human do not hide their sins. Within you operates the principle of the cross, the modus operandi of *strength in weakness*.
>
> This principle points up our problem—we who are religious. We want a Christian reputation more than we want Christ. And yet our Lord, becoming sin for us, "made himself of no reputation." Unlike him we flaunt our successes and hide our failures. . . .
>
> Am I willing to hide my strengths and reveal my weaknesses? Are you? Telling our triumphs, our successes, our achievements, we glorify ourselves. . . . Bragging about my goodness, I build barriers up; when I confess my sins, those barriers come down. . . .
>
> Christ's death frees you from hiding your sins. You can be vulnerable and open. When you are weak then you are strong. You shake the darkness with irresistible blows: the divine might of weakness. You hit your hardest when your guard is down.[5]

Humility

"I forget what is behind." Paul purposely disregarded his past accomplishments as well as the numerous offenses that had been committed against him. This took tremendous humility, especially in light of the kinds of abuses he suffered.

Are they servants of Christ? (I speak as if insane) I

5. Howard Butt, *The Velvet Covered Brick* (New York, N.Y.: Harper and Row, 1973), pp. 41, 43.

more so; in far more labors, in far more imprison-
ments, beaten times without number, often in danger of death. Five times I received from the Jews
thirty-nine lashes. Three times I was beaten with
rods, once I was stoned. (2 Cor. 11:23–25a)

Such cruel wrongs could have consumed Paul, leaving him bitter
and closed; but he chose instead to forgive and forget, to humbly
refuse to keep score, to be bigger than the offenses, and to harbor
no judgmental attitudes.

Perhaps the most memorable Old Testament example of humble
forgetfulness is found in the life of Joseph. Chuck Swindoll recalls
for us Joseph's traumatic injuries and God's grace in his life.

Rejected and hated by his brothers, sold to a group
of travelers in a caravan destined for Egypt, sold
again as a common slave in the Egyptian market,
falsely accused by Potiphar's wife, forgotten in a dun-
geon, and considered dead by his own father, this
man was finally promoted to a position of high authority just beneath the Pharaoh. *If anybody ever had
a reason to nurse his wounds and despise his past, Joseph
was the man!*

But the amazing part of the story is this: He
refused to remember the offenses. In fact, when he
and his wife had their first child, he named the boy
Manasseh, a Hebrew name that meant "forget." He
explains the reason he chose the name:

And Joseph named the first-born Manasseh, "For," he said, "God has made me
forget all my trouble and all my father's
household" (Gen. 41:51).

His words include an extremely important point. In
order for us to forget wrongs done against us, *God*
must do the erasing.

Isaiah, the prophet of Judah, puts it in these
terms:

Fear not, for you will not be put to
shame;
Neither feel humiliated, for you will not

65

be disgraced;
But you will forget the shame of your youth,
And the reproach of your widowhood you
will remember no more.
For your husband is your Maker,
Whose name is the Lord of hosts;
And your redeemer is the Holy One of Israel,
Who is called the God of all the earth
(Isa. 54:4–5).

The Lord God promises us we can forget because He personally will take the place of those painful memories. To you who have had a shameful youth, to you who have lost your mate, the living Lord will replace those awful memories *with Himself*. Great promise! That makes the forgetting possible. Left to ourselves, no way! But with the promise that God will replace the pain with Himself—His presence, His power, His very life—we can "forget what lies behind."[6]

Determination

"I press on." Notice the unstated progression leading up to this statement. First, there had to have been an honest vulnerability— "I am still learning." Second, there naturally followed authentic humility—"I refuse to stay in the past." This then leads to the third step of moving ahead and not quitting—"There are new opportunities to seize in the future." Paul's focus was always on the future; he refused to get bogged down in the past. And because of that, he was able to write near the end of his life, "I have fought the good fight, I have finished the course, I have kept the faith" (2 Tim. 4:7). Now that's the epitaph of someone who chose to forget the past and relentlessly pursue God's objectives for the future.

A Practical Response to Forgetting

Thus far we've spent most of our time defining and describing what it means to be a servant who forgets. The next logical step is to focus our efforts on applying this principle in our own lives. To

---

6. Swindoll, *Improving Your Serve*, pp. 76–77.

help you with this, here are three practical reminders we hope you *won't* forget!

Forgetting reminds me that I, too, have flaws. Remember that if other people kept critical accounts of your every sin and shortcoming, you wouldn't stand a chance. Recognizing this will open you up to forgetting the imperfections of others.

Forgetting enables me to be understanding and encouraging, not petty and negative. By disregarding the faults of others and not holding them against them, you protect your heart from being overrun with a judgmental spirit. More than that, you show a greatheartedness that will inspire others to do the same.

Forgetting frees me to live for tomorrow rather than being hung up on yesterday. We cannot press on toward the tomorrow God desires for us if we're dragging the weight of yesterday along with us.

Living Insights   STUDY ONE

People often misunderstand and misapply the concept of forgetting—with disastrous consequences. So let's be very clear, with the help of Lewis Smedes, about what it really means to forget.

> There are two kinds of pain that we forget. We forget hurts too trivial to bother about. We forget pains too horrible for our memory to manage.
>
> We don't remember every trivial hurt, thank God, not *all* the bruises we have felt from people along the way; if it doesn't go deep, we let it heal itself and we forget.[7]

Let's stop here, on life's multitude of trivial hurts, for our first Living Insight. Isn't forgetting these little things what Paul is referring to in 1 Corinthians 13, where he writes that love "is slow to lose patience. . . . It is not touchy" (vv. 4, 5 PHILLIPS)? Peter also picks up on this idea in his first epistle, saying, "Above all, keep fervent in your love for one another, because love covers a multitude of sins" (1 Pet. 4:8).

The fact is, we all get bumped and scraped every day by minor

---

7. Lewis B. Smedes, *Forgive and Forget: Healing the Hurts We Don't Deserve* (New York, N.Y.: Simon and Schuster Pocket Books, 1984), p. 60.

irritations and petty differences. Those slight cuts, however, can become infected and swollen if we're touchy and quick to anger. That's why Christ wants us to allow our love for Him and for one another to soothe these abrasions so they can quickly heal and be forgotten.

When you've had a minor scrape, do you tend to soothe or swell? Are you the kind of person who is easily provoked? If a waitress is late in refilling your drink, if a grocery clerk accidentally overcharges you fifty cents, or if a driver forgets to signal when turning, do you launch into a tirade covering generations of this other person's family? Or how about, "She didn't look at me"; "He forgot to say, 'Please'"; "They never thanked me"—are these the kinds of little scabs you pick at all day until they become festering wounds?

Some of us have pampered our pet grievances for so long that we wouldn't know how to live without them. We have *become* our trivial injustices.

Is it worth it, letting our lives be nibbled away by such inconsequential irritations as the vacuum cleaner cord not being wound the right way or the lid not being put back on the toothpaste?

Are there some niggling matters you need to let love heal so they can be forgotten? Perhaps a particular one or two that consistently recur? Use the following space to write what comes to mind so that you can begin dealing with them. And don't start nit-picking about there being too much space or not enough or too few lines or . . . just kidding!

☕ *Living Insights*

Forgetting the minor slings and arrows of life out of love for others is right and healthy. Unfortunately, many of us, as Smedes points out, attempt to carry forgetting to an unhealthy extreme—using this method to deal with the "pains too horrible for our memory to manage."

The pains we *dare* not remember are the most dangerous pains of all. We fear to face some horrible thing that once hurt us, and we stuff it into the black holes of our unconsciousness where we suppose it cannot hurt us. But it only comes back disguised; it is like a demon wearing an angel's face. It lays low for a while only to slug us later, on the sly.

Forgetting can be Russian roulette, the same sort of game a woman plays when she "forgets" the little lump she felt on her breast a month ago.

Enough, then, to light up a warning sign: never mistake forgetting for forgiving.

Once we *have* forgiven, however, we get a new freedom to forget. This time forgetting is a sign of health; it is not a trick to avoid spiritual surgery. We *can* forget *because* we have been healed.[8]

When it comes to the deep hurts in your life, are you trying to forget *before* you forgive?

"There is a word," write Dr. David Stoop and Dr. James Masteller,

for what happens when we try to forget painful memories instead of dealing with them straightforwardly. The word is "denial." When we deny what has happened to us, we do not really forget it, in the sense of getting it out of our system entirely. We just pack it up and store it in our emotional deep-freeze. It is like lying to ourselves: by telling ourselves that something bad did not happen—when of course we know that it did—we are only deceiving ourselves.[9]

Before we forget, we must "look the evil full in the face, call it what it is, let its horror shock and stun and enrage us, and only then do we forgive it."[10] Only after we've worked completely

8. Smedes, *Forgive and Forget*, pp. 60–61.

9. David Stoop and James Masteller, *Forgiving Our Parents, Forgiving Ourselves* (Ann Arbor, Mich.: Servant Publications, Vine Books, 1991), p. 189.

10. Smedes, *Forgive and Forget*, p. 107.

through the sometimes long and slow process of forgiving are we capable of forgetting, of letting the harm go and allowing God to heal the damage of that injury.

Is there a specific hurt troubling you right now? Are you attempting to forget because you've forgiven? Or are you forgetting as a way of avoiding facing this problem?

Chapter 9

THINKING LIKE A
SERVANT THINKS
2 Corinthians 10:1–12

Every year people receive renewal notices in the mail for things like magazine subscriptions, license tags, and insurance policies. But the most important item by far that we as servants of Christ will ever renew is our minds. And the renewal notice for that is found in Romans 12:1–2.

> I urge you therefore, brethren, by the mercies of God, to present your bodies a living and holy sacrifice, acceptable to God, which is your spiritual service of worship. And do not be conformed to this world, but be transformed by the renewing of your mind, that you may prove what the will of God is, that which is good and acceptable and perfect.

In *Happiness Is a Choice*, Frank Minirth and Paul Meier explain what this is all about:

> This renewing of the mind is a gradual process that begins at the time of acceptance of Christ . . . and continues throughout life. If the mind has had a substantial amount of bad programming during the early years, it may take many years to reprogram it in a more healthy direction.[1]

Case in point: the first-century Christians in Corinth. Try to imagine the "bad programming" those people were exposed to, while one commentator describes their hometown, Corinth.

> Farrar writes, "Objects of luxury soon found their way to the [Corinthian] markets which were visited by every nation in the civilized world—Arabian balsam, Phoenician dates, Libyan ivory, Babylonian carpets, Cilician goats' hair, Lycaonian wool, Phrygian slaves."

1. Frank B. Minirth and Paul D. Meier, *Happiness Is a Choice* (Grand Rapids, Mich.: Baker Book House, 1978), p. 138.

71

Corinth, as Farrar calls her, was the Vanity Fair of the ancient world. Men called her The Bridge of Greece; one called her The Lounge of Greece. . . . To add to the concourse which came to it, Corinth was the place where the Isthmian Games were held, which were second only to the Olympics. . . .

There was another side to Corinth. She had a reputation for commercial prosperity, but she was also a byword for evil living. The very word *korinthiazesthai*, to live like a Corinthian, had become a part of the Greek language, and meant to live with drunken and immoral debauchery. . . . There was one source of evil in the city which was known all over the civilized world. Above the isthmus towered the hill of the Acropolis, and on it stood the great temple of Aphrodite, the goddess of love. To that temple there were attached one thousand priestesses who were sacred prostitutes, and in the evenings they descended from the Acropolis and plied their trade upon the streets of Corinth. . . . In addition to these cruder sins, there flourished far more recondite vices, which had come in with the traders and the sailors from the ends of the earth, until Corinth became not only a synonym for wealth and luxury, drunkenness and debauchery, but also for filth.[2]

Is it any wonder those who became Christians in that city were perhaps the most self-centered, worldly-minded bunch of babes in Christ ever to form a church? Corinth's carnal hopes, speculations, reasonings, values, impulses, and opinions were deeply ingrained in each of them. So how were they supposed to accomplish the impossible and transform their lives into living and holy sacrifices acceptable to God?

Larry Crabb gives us the answer. "Transformation," he writes, "depends on renewing not our feelings, not our behavior, not our circumstances, but our minds."[3]

2. William Barclay, *The Letters to the Corinthians*, rev. ed., The Daily Study Bible Series (Philadelphia, Pa.: Westminster Press, 1975), pp. 2–3.

3. Lawrence J. Crabb Jr., *Effective Biblical Counseling* (Grand Rapids, Mich.: Zondervan Publishing House, 1977), p. 139.

To learn more about renewing our minds so that we think like a servant of God, let's eavesdrop on the apostle Paul as he confronts the Corinthians' unrenewed thinking concerning his authenticity and authority as an apostle.

Natural Thinking in Today's World

In 2 Corinthians 10, Paul digs in to defend himself against criticisms leveled by some false apostles in the church at Corinth. So strong was their antagonism and influence that "Paul believed that the danger of people defecting from him and his gospel was decidedly real."[4] And though we're not told what the specific charges were, we can infer from Paul's defense four characteristics of the Corinthians' unrenewed thinking that are also common today.

First, *they were prejudiced instead of objective.*

> I plead with you—yes, I, Paul—and I plead gently, as Christ himself would do. Yet some of you are saying, "Paul's letters are bold enough when he is far away, but when he gets here he will be afraid to raise his voice!"
> I hope I won't need to show you when I come how harsh and rough I can be. I don't want to carry out my present plans against some of you who seem to think my deeds and words are merely those of an ordinary man. (vv. 1–2 LB)

Apparently, a rumor was circulating that Paul's bark was worse than his bite. His letters are bold, the critics said, but his personal presence is "unimpressive, and his speech contemptible" (v. 10). Unimpressive, contemptible? Such words were enough to cause many to lose their objectivity and become prejudiced against Paul, deciding, "He must be a fake."

Second, *they focused on the visible rather than the invisible.*

> It is true that I am an ordinary, weak human being, but I don't use human plans and methods to win my battles. . . .

4. David K. Lowery, "2 Corinthians," *The Bible Knowledge Commentary*, New Testament ed. (Wheaton, Ill.: Scripture Press Publications, Victor Books, 1983), p. 576.

> The trouble with you is that you look at me and I seem weak and powerless, but you don't look beneath the surface. Yet if anyone can claim the power and authority of Christ, I certainly can. (vv. 3, 7 LB)

Paul's focus on the invisible was totally opposite the natural thinking of the unrenewed mind, which focused exclusively on outward appearances. Wasn't that what the Corinthians were doing, judging him by his physical stature and rhetorical skills?[5]

Third, *they relied on human strength rather than divine power.*

> I use God's mighty weapons, not those made by men, to knock down the devil's strongholds. (v. 4 LB)

Paul depended on divinely powerful weapons for spiritual warfare. The natural mind, however, puts its trust in human strength and skill—weapons that have no power in the spiritual realm of conflict. Francis Schaeffer included a sobering illustration of this very point in his book *No Little People.*

> Imagine the devil or a demon entering your room right now. You have a sword by your side, so when you see him you rush at him and stab him. But the sword passes straight through and doesn't faze him! The most awesome modern weapon you could think of could not destroy him. Whenever we do the Lord's work in the flesh, our strokes "pass right through" because we do not battle earthly forces.[6]

And fourth, *they listened to people rather than God.*

> These weapons can break down every proud argument against God and every wall that can be built to keep men from finding him. With these weapons I can capture rebels and bring them back to God, and change them into men whose hearts' desire is obedience to Christ. (v. 5 LB)

Paul was sensitive to God's voice. The Corinthians, however, allowed themselves to be swayed by the subtle voices of the false apostles.

---

5. Compare 1 Samuel 16:7.

6. Francis A. Schaeffer, *No Little People* (Downers Grove, Ill.: InterVarsity Press, 1974), p. 71.

In addition to these patterns of unrenewed thinking, we all have erected certain mental barriers that block the renewal of our minds. Returning to verses 4–5, let's dig a little deeper to discover four obstacles each of us must overcome in order to think like a servant.

Mental Barriers to God's Voice

Before we examine the obstacles Paul mentions, it will help to understand the way ancient cities were fortified. To withstand attack, cities were enclosed with high, wide, formidable walls. Next, guards were posted for constant surveillance. Last, high towers were built inside the city so that military strategists could direct their troops to effectively counter the attack of any enemy.

Now let's read with fresh understanding Paul's analogy between a fortified city and our minds.

> For the weapons of our warfare are not of the flesh, but divinely powerful for the destruction of fortresses. We are destroying speculations and every lofty thing raised up against the knowledge of God, and we are taking every thought captive to the obedience of Christ. (vv. 4–5)

In effect, Paul says that when the Spirit comes to renew our thinking, He must scale four fortifications of the mind.

First: *the wall, our mental "fortress."* As the Spirit advances on our minds with His truth, He runs up against a wall—our general attitude toward life. For some, this natural mind-set is prejudice. For others, it's limited or negative thinking. And for still others, it is humanistic philosophy. "Whatever, it is a huge mental barrier that resists divine input just as firmly as a massive stone wall once resisted the invading troops."[7]

Second: *the guards, our mental "speculations."* These are the defense mechanisms we employ to guard ourselves from the Spirit's forward movement. Two such guards, Blaming and Self-Justification, fight with a passion to protect our ingrained thinking.

Third: *the towers, our mental "lofty things."* Reinforcing the mind's defenses are its lofty towers of pride. These may appear as an unteachable, argumentative, antagonistic spirit and a stubborn

---

7. Charles R. Swindoll, *Improving Your Serve: The Art of Unselfish Living* (Waco, Tex.: Word Books Publisher, 1981), p. 87.

unwillingness to change. For God to take control of our minds, these, too, must be torn down and kept from being built back up.

Fourth: *the strategists, our mental "thoughts."* Our strategists are those techniques we use to repel God's Word and His promptings. We all have them—predetermined plans of attack and evasion, ready at a moment's notice to protect our pride. These must be replaced with new strategies designed to promote Christ instead.

Supernatural Ability of the "Renewed Mind"

In minds where the barriers have been replaced with God's truth, several important characteristics surface that are readily visible in the apostle Paul. For instance, *courage against odds* (vv. 2–3). You get the distinct impression from his words—*war, weapons, warfare, destruction, taking captive, punish*—that a renewed mind is unintimidated! Why? Because God is behind it, protecting and guiding. And, as Paul wrote in Romans 8:31, "If God is for us, who is against us?"

Another benefit is *divine power* (2 Cor. 10:4). Servants who renew their minds with God's truth gain a more secure and sound perspective on life.

A third ability is a desire to be *obedient to Christ* (v. 5). Every new device, each new technique, honors Christ rather than fights Him.

A final trait to note, *authenticity*, is found in verses 11–12.

> Let such a person consider this, that what we are in word by letters when absent, such persons we are also in deed when present. For we are not bold to class or compare ourselves with some of those who commend themselves; but when they measure themselves by themselves, and compare themselves with themselves, they are without understanding.

The Apostle wore no mask of hypocrisy. He didn't claim to be one kind of person when in reality he was another. The man the Corinthians saw in Paul's letters was the same man they would see when he came to them in person. In addition, Paul reflects the truth that the renewed mind doesn't base its worth on comparisons with others.

Servanthood Starts in the Mind

Like the Corinthians, we also need to renew our minds. But

how? Here are two essential steps. First, *operating from a renewed mind begins with a decision.* Renewal won't happen simply because we go to church. We can hear the best sermons, sing the most beautiful hymns, but until we commit to renewing our minds, our thinking, our lives will remain basically unchanged.

And second, *continuing to operate from a renewed mind is a daily issue.* Being transformed is a process. Our minds are heavily guarded and do not easily surrender to the truth of the Holy Spirit. Thus, ground gained one day can easily be lost the next if we don't continuously fight the good fight of faith.

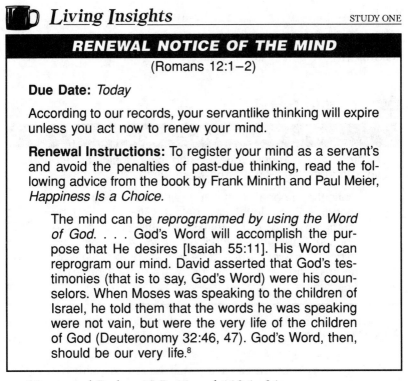

□ Living Insights

RENEWAL NOTICE OF THE MIND
(Romans 12:1–2)

Due Date: *Today*

According to our records, your servantlike thinking will expire unless you act now to renew your mind.

Renewal Instructions: To register your mind as a servant's and avoid the penalties of past-due thinking, read the following advice from the book by Frank Minirth and Paul Meier, *Happiness Is a Choice.*

> The mind can be *reprogrammed by using the Word of God.* . . . God's Word will accomplish the purpose that He desires [Isaiah 55:11]. His Word can reprogram our mind. David asserted that God's testimonies (that is to say, God's Word) were his counselors. When Moses was speaking to the children of Israel, he told them that the words he was speaking were not vain, but were the very life of the children of God (Deuteronomy 32:46, 47). God's Word, then, should be our very life.[8]

Next, read Psalms 19:7–11 and 119:1–24.

Do you really believe what these psalms are saying about God's Word—that it can restore the soul, make the simple wise, rejoice

8. Minirth and Meier, *Happiness Is a Choice*, pp. 138–39.

the heart, and keep your way pure? Then will you make a commitment to renew your mind by diligently studying and treasuring God's Word in your heart on a regular basis?

To register your renewal form, simply notify God in a prayer addressed to "My Father, who art in heaven." Then use the space provided to set aside a specific time each day in the coming week to renew your mind in His Word.

Personal Study Schedule

Monday _____   Thursday _____

Tuesday _____   Friday _____

Wednesday _____   Saturday _____

Don't stop with this week! Get your calendar to help you in making this a regular part of your changing life.

☕ *Living Insights*   STUDY TWO

RENEWAL NOTICE ADDENDUM

Another way to renew your thinking is by closely monitoring your thought life. Minirth and Meier write,

> Critical and negative thinking reinforces a depressed mood. An individual can help to lift his mood by changing the way he thinks. In Philippians 4:8 the apostle Paul encouraged his readers to think on things that were true, honest, just, pure, lovely, of good report, and things that were worthy of virtue and praise.[9]

What kind of thoughts has your mind been preoccupied with today? Have they been negative and critical or were they pure and lovely?

Taking every thought captive to Christ is a constant battle. We cannot let our guard down for even a moment at work, at home, or at play. Stay alert. Pray for God's sensitivity to immediately recognize a destructive thought so that you can stop it before it has

---

9. Minirth and Meier, *Happiness Is a Choice*, p. 139.

a chance to advance and overtake your mind.

In addition to prayer, what other practical ideas can you think of that might help you monitor your mind?

_____

_____

_____

_____

_____

Chapter 10

PORTRAIT OF A SERVANT
(PART ONE)
Matthew 5:1–12

John Stott, well-known teacher and author, has called the Sermon on the Mount "probably the best-known part of the teaching of Jesus, though arguably it is the least understood, and certainly it is the least obeyed. It is the nearest thing to a manifesto that he ever uttered, for it is his own description of what he wanted his followers to be and to do."[1]

And what does Jesus want His followers to be? In a word—*different*.

Stott continues:

> Jesus emphasized that his true followers . . . were to be entirely different from others. They were not to take their cue from the people around them, but from him, and so prove to be genuine children of their heavenly Father. To me the key text of the Sermon on the Mount is 6:8: "Do not be like them." It is immediately reminiscent of God's word to Israel in olden days: "You shall not do as they do." It is the same call. . . .
>
> Thus the followers of Jesus are to be different— different from both the nominal church and the secular world, different from both the religious and the irreligious. The Sermon on the Mount is the most complete delineation anywhere in the New Testament of the Christian counter-culture. Here is a Christian value-system, ethical standard, religious devotion, attitude to money, ambition, life-style and network of relationships—all of which are totally at variance with those of the non-Christian world.[2]

For a deeper understanding of what it means to be different as

---

1. John R. W. Stott, *The Message of the Sermon on the Mount (Matthew 5–7): Christian Counter-Culture* (Downers Grove, Ill.: Inter-Varsity Press, 1978), p. 15.

2. Stott, *Sermon on the Mount,* pp. 18–19.

servants of Christ, let's focus our attention on the opening section of Jesus' sermon—the Beatitudes.

The Beatitudes: Three Observations

Using eight brush strokes rich in diversity and depth, Jesus leaves us a portrait in Matthew 5:1–12 that is next to impossible to take in at one sitting. We can, however, note three characteristics that are true for each facet.

First: *Each identifies true servants.* With each new "Blessed are the . . . ," the curtains are pulled back a little farther to give us a broader perspective on the traits of an authentic servant—traits, by the way, that every Christian should cultivate. And not just one or two, mind you, but all eight. We cannot pick and choose from Jesus' teaching as if He were offering the Beatitudes in a buffet line.

Second: *Each opens the door to inner happiness.* "Blessed . . . blessed . . . blessed . . ." This is the only time in Christ's teachings where He repeats the same term eight times (vv. 3–10). It's another way of saying, "Oh how happy, how satisfied and fulfilled will the person be who models these fundamental attitudes."[3]

Third: *Each has a corresponding promise.* If you pause for a moment to glance over the Beatitudes, you'll notice that each has the same basic structure: "Blessed are . . . (the trait), for . . . (the promise)." Jesus sets forth a particular benefit for each particular quality. And if you take the time to study those promises, you'll have no difficulty understanding why this series of attitudes will lead to true happiness.

An Analysis of Four Beatitudes

Since the wisdom of the Beatitudes is so richly concentrated, we'll limit our study in this chapter to examining only the first four. Let's observe Jesus' words carefully so that we might reproduce every shade of their meaning in our own lives.

The Poor in Spirit

"Blessed are the poor in spirit, for theirs is the

---

3. *Blessed* comes from the Greek term *makarios*, which, according to William Barclay, means "that joy which is serene and untouchable, and self-contained, that joy which is completely independent of all the chances and changes of life." *The Gospel of Matthew,* vol. 1, rev. ed., The Daily Study Bible Series (Philadelphia, Pa.: Westminster Press, 1975), p. 89. Used by kind permission of The Saint Andrew Press, Edinburgh, Scotland.

kingdom of heaven." (v. 3)

On the surface, it appears as if Jesus is saying, "Happy are those who have little or no money to pay their bills or buy food." But actually, He's not talking about the poor in the pocketbook, rather the "poor *in spirit*" (emphasis added). William Barclay clarifies the meaning of this kind of poverty by tracing its historical roots in Jewish culture.

> The Jews had a special way of using the word *Poor.* In Hebrew the word is *'ani* or *ebiōn.* These words in Hebrew underwent a four-stage development of meaning. (i) They began by meaning simply poor. (ii) They went on to mean, *because poor, therefore having no influence or power, or help, or prestige.* (iii) They went on to mean, *because having no influence, therefore down-trodden and oppressed by men.* (iv) Finally, they came to describe *the man who, because he has no earthly resources whatever, puts his whole trust in God. . . .*
>
> . . . Therefore, "Blessed are the poor in spirit" means:
>
> > Blessed is the man who has realised his own utter helplessness, and who has put his whole trust in God.[4]

The indispensable condition for receiving the promised kingdom of heaven is acknowledging our own spiritual poverty. Even those who have already confessed that poverty and received salvation through faith in Christ must earnestly continue to cultivate this attitude. To neglect it is to invite the same kind of self-sufficient complacency that nauseated the Lord about the church in Laodicea.

> "I know your deeds, that you are neither cold nor hot; I would that you were cold or hot. So because you are lukewarm, and neither hot nor cold, I will spit you out of My mouth. Because you say, 'I am rich, and have become wealthy, and have need of nothing,' and you do not know that you are wretched and miserable and poor and blind and naked." (Rev. 3:15–17)

4. Barclay, *The Gospel of Matthew*, p. 91.

Acknowledging our own neediness is the humble birthplace of authentic servanthood.

Those Who Mourn

> "Blessed are those who mourn, for they shall be comforted." (Matt. 5:4)

The word used here for *mourn*, according to William Barclay, "is the strongest word for mourning in the Greek language. It is the word which is used for mourning for the dead, for the passionate lament for one who was loved."[5] Such grief conveys a deep sorrowing in the heart, an abiding ache of the soul over cruelties in the world, a shattering personal loss, or one's own destructive sinfulness.

At the core of this character trait is the picture of someone with a compassionate heart. Paraphrased, the beatitude might read, "Blessed is the man who cares intensely for the sufferings, and for the sorrows, and for the needs of others."[6] Servants who manifest this trait, Christ promises, "shall be comforted." Exactly how or by whom, we're not told; we only know that comfort *will* come. Perhaps from the very same people to whom the servant has shown compassion (see Prov. 11:25).

The Gentle

> "Blessed are the gentle, for they shall inherit the earth." (Matt. 5:5)

Many have sarcastically interpreted this to say, "Blessed are the weak, for they shall be walked on by others." Why? Because the word *gentle*, or *meek*, as the old King James Version puts it, is often perceived as meaning someone who is feeble, effeminate, and spineless. In Jesus' day, however, the Greek term for *gentle* denoted strength under control, like a wild stallion which has been tamed. It can also mean:

- Carefully chosen words that soothe strong emotions
- Ointment that takes the sting out of a wound
- Tenderness with those who are afraid or in pain

5. Barclay, *The Gospel of Matthew*, p. 93.
6. Barclay, *The Gospel of Matthew*, pp. 94–95.

- A sense of politeness, tact, courtesy, and respect

Paraphrased, the beatitude might read, "How happy are those servants who respect others by dealing carefully with their feelings, listening closely to their words, and calming those who are uncontrolled." For they shall—"inherit the earth."

To many Christians who struggle to get by while so many ruthless people prosper, the promise of inheriting the earth seems hard to believe. We don't often see it happening now, so we wonder, *When* will this inheritance be ours to enjoy? The answer is really twofold. Literal fulfillment will ultimately come in the future, as David reassures us in Psalm 37; but figurative fulfillment can also happen in the present. Commentator James Boice explains:

> There is a sense in which the [gentle] shall inherit the earth now. For the [gentle] man is the man who is satisfied and is therefore content. Paul was such a man. He owned very little, yet he spoke of himself as "possessing all things" (2 Cor. 6:10). He wrote to the contentious Corinthians: "Therefore, let no man glory in men. For all things are yours, whether Paul, or Apollos, or Cephas, or the world, or life, or death, or things present, or things to come; all are yours, and ye are Christ's, and Christ is God's" (1 Cor. 3:21–23).[7]

Those Who Hunger and Thirst for Righteousness

> "Blessed are those who hunger and thirst for righteousness, for they shall be satisfied." (Matt. 5:6)

The final trait discussed in this chapter includes what we might call survival appetites—hunger and thirst. Just as both these drives are basic to our physical survival, so they are also essential to our spiritual growth. The servant is to have a passionate appetite for righteousness, a heart that clings to the Lord (see 2 Kings 18:5–6). This clinging, or cleaving (compare Gen. 2:24), according to Frank Minirth and Paul Meier,

> implies a friendship. It implies a longing to be with someone. It implies enjoyment in being with that

7. James Montgomery Boice, *The Sermon on the Mount* (Grand Rapids, Mich.: Zondervan Publishing House, Ministry Resources Library, 1972), p. 41.

someone, and it implies spending much time together. To cleave to God implies that we are intensely in pursuit of Him. It means that we desire
to spend time with Him, to walk with Him and talk
with Him, to know Him as we would any other
friend, and to be close to Him.[8]

Hungering and thirsting after righteousness, however, is not
limited to just looking upward and longing for holiness. It also
involves looking around and being grieved over the corruption, the
inequities, and the moral compromises that abound—and wanting
to live in a way that stands against the wrongs in life.

For those who possess such a passionate appetite for vertical
and horizontal righteousness, Jesus promises, "they shall be satisfied." According to Greek scholar A. T. Robertson, the term for
satisfied comes from the word *fodder* or *grass*, meaning to feed and
fatten cattle.[9] It's a familiar word picture of contentment. The servant who hungers and thirsts for righteousness will find those appetites abundantly satisfied and slaked in Christ (also compare
Phil. 4:11–13).

Preliminary Questions to Answer

Before going on to examine the final four Beatitudes in the next
chapter, let's pause briefly to ask ourselves three hard but necessary
questions.

- Is my lifestyle any different from the world around me?

- Do I care? Do I take what Jesus is saying seriously enough to
  wrestle with it and change?

- What significant impact will the ideas from these first four Beatitudes have on my life today?

8. Frank B. Minirth and Paul D. Meier, *Happiness Is a Choice* (Grand Rapids, Mich.: Baker
Book House, 1978), p. 140.

9. Archibald Thomas Robertson, *Word Pictures in the New Testament* (Grand Rapids, Mich.:
Baker Book House, 1930), vol. 1, p. 41.

☕ _Living Insights_

Let's go back to those uncomfortable questions at the end of the chapter—the ones most of us probably skimmed over—and take a deeper look at the first one.

Are you different? If you were to strip away all the "spiritual" activities, like attending church and Bible studies, and got rid of the plaques and T-shirts with Scripture on them, would people still notice a difference about your life? Would there be a discernible discrepancy between you and the person next door who doesn't know Christ?

The sad truth is that many of us measure our difference as Christians solely by outward appearances. Jesus, however, draws His conclusions by examining our hearts to see if we're poor in spirit, compassionate, gentle, and thirsting for righteousness. These are the differences He notices—and the world does too. We only fool ourselves if we think that not drinking or swearing is enough to convince people we're different, while in our hearts we remain poor, blind, and naked in our pride just as the Laodiceans in Revelation 3.

Are you different, really? Before you answer that question, take a look in the mirror of the four attitudes studied in this chapter and see how much of you is reflected in each of them.

☕ _Living Insights_

Putting on a beatitude is not like trying on a shirt or a pair of shoes. We can't just simply decide, "Today I think I'll wear my poor-in-spirit attitude and for tomorrow . . . hmm, let's see, how about gentle? No, no that'll definitely clash with the business meetings I have planned. Oh, I know—mourning! Everybody loved my compassion-coordinated look the last time I wore it."

Sounds ridiculous, doesn't it? Yet some Christians attempt to put on the Beatitudes just like that, almost as if they were playing dress-up. Qualities like hungering and thirsting for righteousness, however, are tailor-made to fit only the inner man. So how do we "put on" this new self Jesus describes? The same way we learned as children to button our own shirts and tie our own shoes—practice. Yes, it can be frustrating and slow at times, but the apostle Paul says:

> Therefore we do not lose heart, but though our

outer man is decaying, yet our inner man is being renewed day by day. (2 Cor. 4:16)

The more we practice the Beatitudes day by day, the less these attitudes will be something we consciously put on and more something we have become.

What are some specific situations currently going on at work, with a friend, or at home where the four qualities from our lesson could be practiced this week? Use the space provided to write out your thoughts concerning each one.

Poverty of Spirit: _____

_____

_____

Mourning: _____

_____

_____

Gentleness: _____

_____

_____

Hunger and Thirst for Righteousness: _____

_____

_____

Chapter 11

PORTRAIT OF A SERVANT
(PART TWO)
Matthew 5:1–12

What do you want to be when you grow up?"

Of all the questions children are asked, this one is perhaps the most widely known and most oft repeated. Art Linkletter used it regularly, with hilarious results, as he interviewed the unfettered minds of youngsters on his 1950's TV show "House Party." For example, when asked this same question, one boy replied with religious conviction,

> "I want to be a missionary . . . and preach in Africa."
>
> "That's difficult work," [Art] cautioned. "Why did you pick Africa?"
>
> "'Cause they have big crocodiles down there and if the people don't listen to me I can sic the crocodiles on them!"[1]

Fortunately for the folks in Africa, few of us ever end up doing exactly what we dreamed about when we were little. But suppose for just a moment that we did. What do you think God would want all of us to dream about becoming? *Servants*—of course. Whether we live in Africa or America, whether we're missionaries or mechanics, the Lord Jesus desires that we be different. And He's been defining that difference for us in His Sermon on the Mount.

Analysis of Four More Qualities

Let's continue our study of the Beatitudes in Matthew 5, this time focusing on the final four traits that define what a servant is and what we should be when we grow up.

The Merciful

> "Blessed are the merciful, for they shall receive mercy." (v. 7)

1. Art Linkletter, *Kids Say the Damdest Things!* (Englewood Cliffs, N.J.: Prentice-Hall, 1957), p. 25.

Mercy is compassion for people in need. It is concern for those who hurt, who suffer the misery of pain, distress, and sorrow. But mercy goes deeper than just feeling sorry for someone in trouble. As William Barclay explains, it means

> the ability to get right inside the other person's skin until we can see things with his eyes, think things with his mind, and feel things with his feelings.
>
> Clearly this is much more than an emotional wave of pity; clearly this demands a quite deliberate effort of the mind and of the will. It denotes a sympathy which is not given, as it were, from outside, but which comes from a deliberate identification with the other person, until we see things as he sees them, and feel things as he feels them.[2]

John Howard Griffin did just this back in 1959 when he shaved his hair and darkened his skin and became, for a time, as a black man in the South. In his book *Black like Me*, he retells "the changes that occur to heart and body and intelligence when a so-called first-class citizen is cast on the junkheap of second-class citizenship."[3] He'd felt sympathy for black people before, but not until he was "inside their skin" did he really know and understand the horror of bigotry.

That's where mercy is born, out of the womb of identification. For Jesus, it was the literal womb of a young Jewish girl that made it possible for Him to get inside our skin and experience our weaknesses, as the author of Hebrews confirms:

> Since then we have a great high priest who has passed through the heavens, Jesus the Son of God, let us hold fast our confession. For we do not have a high priest who cannot sympathize with our weaknesses, but one who has been tempted in all things as we are, yet without sin. (Heb. 4:14–15)

The beautiful promise Jesus gives to those who show mercy is

2. William Barclay, *The Gospel of Matthew*, vol. 1, rev. ed., The Daily Study Bible Series (Philadelphia, Pa.: Westminster Press, 1975), p. 103. Used by kind permission of The Saint Andrew Press, Edinburgh, Scotland.

3. John Howard Griffin, *Black like Me*, 2d ed. (Boston, Mass.: Houghton Mifflin Co., 1977), preface.

that they will receive mercy in return. Get involved in the lives of others, comfort them in their hurts and disappointments, and they, too, will be more likely to have compassion on you in times of sorrow and pain.

The Pure in Heart

> "Blessed are the pure in heart, for they shall see God." (Matt. 5:8)

The key to understanding this verse is that small phrase "in heart." It doesn't refer simply to those who do the right things, but to those who do the right things for the right reasons. A servant is to be free from hypocrisy, duplicity, and sham. Jesus' fiercest criticism fell on the Pharisees because they pretended to honor God with their lip service while their hearts were far away from Him (see 15:7–9).

Perhaps His most blistering confrontation with the Pharisees is found in Matthew 23. Unlike the eight "Blessed are you" phrases of the Beatitudes, this chapter contains eight "Woe to you" warnings. Two, in particular, deal directly with the Pharisees' empty religion, their lack of purity in heart.

> "Woe to you, scribes and Pharisees, hypocrites! For you clean the outside of the cup and of the dish, but inside they are full of robbery and self-indulgence. You blind Pharisee, first clean the inside of the cup and of the dish, so that the outside of it may become clean also.
> "Woe to you, scribes and Pharisees, hypocrites! For you are like whitewashed tombs which on the outside appear beautiful, but inside they are full of dead men's bones and all uncleanness. Even so you too outwardly appear righteous to men, but inwardly you are full of hypocrisy and lawlessness." (vv. 25–28)

In contrast to the unclean hearts of the Pharisees, Jesus uses one word back in Matthew 5:8 to describe the heart of a servant—"pure." The Greek word for *pure*, according to Barclay, has several usages,

> all of which have something to add to the meaning of this beatitude.
> (i) Originally [the word] simply meant *clean*, and could, for instance, be used of soiled clothes which

90

have been washed clean.

(ii) It is regularly used for corn which has been winnowed or sifted and cleansed of all chaff. In the same way it is used of an army which has been purged of all discontented, cowardly, unwilling and inefficient soldiers, and which is a force composed solely of first-class fighting men.

(iii) It very commonly appears in company with another Greek adjective—*akēratos*. *Akēratos* can be used of milk or wine which is unadulterated with water, or of metal which has in it no tinge of alloy.

So, then, the basic meaning of [*pure*] is *unmixed, unadulterated, unalloyed*. That is why this beatitude is so demanding a beatitude. It could be translated:

> Blessed is the man whose motives are always entirely unmixed, for that man shall see God. . . .

This beatitude demands from us the most exacting self-examination. Is our work done from motives of service or from motives of pay? Is our service given from selfless motives or from motives of self-display? Is the work we do in Church done for Christ or for our own prestige?[4]

And what is our reward for such a demanding self-examination? We shall see God, "see him now with the eye of faith," writes John Stott, "and see his glory in the hereafter, for only the utterly sincere can bear the dazzling vision in whose light the darkness of deceit must vanish and by whose fire all shams are burned up."[5]

The Peacemakers

> "Blessed are the peacemakers, for they shall be called sons of God." (v. 9)

This is the only time in the New Testament that the Greek term for *peacemakers* appears. To clarify its meaning, let's first

---

4. Barclay, *The Gospel of Matthew*, pp. 106-7.

5. John R. W. Stott, *The Message of the Sermon on the Mount (Matthew 5-7): Christian Counter-Culture* (Downers Grove, Ill.: Inter-Varsity Press, 1978), p. 49.

identify what this word does not communicate. For example, it doesn't mean

- Avoiding all conflicts and confrontations,
- Being easygoing and relaxed,
- Defending a peace-at-any-price philosophy,
- Being passive about any controversial issue.

If not these, then what? Let's let the Scriptures speak for themselves before we draw any conclusions.

> Seek peace, and pursue it. (Ps. 34:14b)

> If possible, so far as it depends on you, be at peace with all men. (Rom. 12:18)

> So then let us pursue the things which make for peace and the building up of one another. (14:19)

> For where jealousy and selfish ambition exist, there is disorder and every evil thing. But the wisdom from above is first pure, then peaceable, gentle, reasonable, full of mercy and good fruits, unwavering, without hypocrisy. And the seed whose fruit is righteousness is sown in peace by those who make peace. (James 3:16–18)

Even from this brief overview, the imperative for Christ's servants is clear—make peace! To do that, we must first be at peace with ourselves, at ease internally, not agitated and abrasive. Second, we must strive to settle quarrels rather than start them. Third, we must be constructive and positive with our words rather than destructive and negative. Solomon describes for us the language of a peacemaker.

> A gentle answer turns away wrath,
> But a harsh word stirs up anger. . . .
> Pleasant words are a honeycomb,
> Sweet to the soul and healing to the bones. . . .
> Like apples of gold in settings of silver
> Is a word spoken in right circumstances.
> (Prov. 15:1; 16:24; 25:11)

In every church there are troublemakers and peacemakers.

"There are people," writes Barclay,

> who are always storm-centres of trouble and bitter-
> ness and strife. . . . On the other hand—thank
> God—there are people in whose presence bitterness
> cannot live, people who bridge the gulfs, and heal
> the breaches. . . . Such people are doing a godlike
> work, for it is the great purpose of God to bring
> peace between men and himself, and between man
> and man.[6]

Because peacemakers do the work of God, they shall be called,
Jesus promises, "sons of God."

The Persecuted

> "Blessed are those who have been persecuted for
> the sake of righteousness, for theirs is the kingdom
> of heaven. Blessed are you when men cast insults at
> you, and persecute you, and say all kinds of evil
> against you falsely, on account of me. Rejoice, and
> be glad, for your reward in heaven is great, for so
> they persecuted the prophets who were before you."
> (Matt. 5:10–12)

Coming after peacemaking, Jesus' focus here on persecution may
seem out of place. But it's not misplaced—it's realistic. The truth
is, people who do right are often treated wrongly. It can happen
because of misunderstanding or just plain mean-spiritedness. Either
way, it's mistreatment directed at someone who does not deserve
it. And the only way to endure it at times is to look beyond the
present pain to the great rewards Jesus promises in the future.

In his book *Improving Your Serve*, Chuck Swindoll tells the story
of how this beatitude steadied and strengthened a well-known servant of the nineteenth century, Charles Haddon Spurgeon.

Extremely popular and gifted of God, Spurgeon nevertheless
had his share of jousts with critical detractors. Normally he could
withstand these attacks, his resilient spirit buoying him up. But one
time they became too much, and he began to falter and slump. His
wife, seeing the effect of these cruel blows, decided to take action
in helping him regain his strength. Printing out the words of this

---

6. Barclay, *The Gospel of Matthew*, p. 110.

last beatitude, she then tacked the message to the ceiling above Spurgeon's side of the bed.

> Every morning, every evening, when he would rest his enormous frame in his bed, the words were there to meet and to encourage him.
> Blessed are those who have been persecuted for the sake of righteousness. . . .
> The large sheet of paper remained fixed to the ceiling for an extended period of time until it had done the job.[7]

Of course, Spurgeon could have sicced crocodiles on his detractors, like the little boy who wanted to be a missionary; but he chose, instead, to be a servant and focus on his future rewards. What will your approach to persecution be?

A Last Look at the Portrait

We've studied in close detail each of the eight Beatitudes presented in Matthew 5. Combined, they form a grand portrait of servanthood, of what Jesus wants us to be when we grow up. Step up close and look one last time at each of the qualities: poor in spirit, mourning, gentle, hungering and thirsting for righteousness, merciful, pure in heart, peacemakers, persecuted. Memorize their individual nuances and shapes. Imitate their emphases. Internalize their truths until your servanthood becomes as authentic as the Master's, whose signature is on this portrait.

Living Insights   STUDY ONE

Imagine for a moment that you're eavesdropping on a pastoral search committee interviewing two potential candidates.

Committee Chairperson: "Would you both share your philosophy about helping those in need?"

Candidate #1: "Oh, I feel deeply for those less fortunate souls who are destitute. It just makes me weep every time I pass by someone living on the street. (The committee members nod their

---

7. Charles R. Swindoll, *Improving Your Serve: The Art of Unselfish Living* (Waco, Tex.: Word Books Publisher, 1981), p. 122.

heads in approval and sigh empathetically.) My wife has often told others that she feels I have a special sensitivity, an anointing, if you will, to the hurts and trials of the poor. (More nods and a "Praise the Lord.") In gratitude for this special gift, I have covenanted with the Lord to sacrifice five minutes every day on my knees beseeching the Almighty on behalf of all the hungry and homeless in the world."

Chairperson: (Everyone is smiling and impressed except the second candidate, who looks a little annoyed.) "Blessed are the merciful, brother. I believe we're all touched by your example. And, now, let's hear from our second candidate. What is your philosophy about helping the poor?"

Candidate #2: "My philosophy is simple. If a man or woman is without clothing or food and you say, 'I'm touched by your suffering and promise to pray for you. God bless, go in peace'—what good is that? (Dead silence.) It shouldn't take a special anointing to realize that mere words are not true mercy. True mercy is practical, it feeds and clothes the poor, comforts the sick, and cares for the elderly. We're to be doers of mercy, not merely talkers who delude themselves." (More silence.)

Chairperson: "Uh, well (clears throat), of course we would all agree with you. But I think that, perhaps, our first candidate will be better suited to meet the needs of this church. Go in peace, be warmed and be filled."

Guess who just got turned down? You're right, the apostle of practicality—James. If he were alive today and this had been a real interview, he probably wouldn't have gotten the job in a lot of churches. His frankness offends too many people. His view of mercy is too messy, too involved . . .

. . . but it is right. And one day Jesus will have some frank words of His own to say to those of us whose mercy has been miserly.

> "But when the Son of Man comes in His glory, and all the angels with Him, then He will sit on His glorious throne. And all the nations will be gathered before Him; and He will separate them from one another, as the shepherd separates the sheep from the goats; and He will put the sheep on His right, and the goats on the left. . . . Then He will . . . say to those on His left, 'Depart from Me, accursed ones, into the eternal fire which has been prepared

for the devil and his angels; for I was hungry, and you gave Me nothing to eat; I was thirsty, and you gave Me nothing to drink; I was a stranger, and you did not invite Me in; naked, and you did not clothe Me; sick, and in prison, and you did not visit Me.' Then they themselves also will answer, saying, 'Lord, when did we see You hungry, or thirsty, or a stranger, or naked, or sick, or in prison, and did not take care of You?' Then He will answer them saying, 'Truly I say to you, to the extent that you did not do it to one of the least of these, you did not do it to Me.'" (Matt. 25:31–33, 41–46)

The true measure of our mercy is not our words but our deeds. This week, be a doer and give Jesus something to eat, invite Him into your home, give Him something to wear, drive Him to that job interview, visit Him in that hospital. Get involved. Make plans to minister to Him on a regular basis.

📖 *Living Insights*

"Blessed are those who have been persecuted for the sake of righteousness." (Matt. 5:10a)

Being made fun of and maligned for doing what is right can be a horrendous experience. One that can leave you, at times, doubting yourself, your motives, even your faith in the Lord. Persecution does that so powerfully. It can subtly twist your perspective around enough to even make you accuse yourself over past sins and wonder, Is God punishing me for something?

If you've been there, you know how disorienting and disheartening unjust suffering can be. And you may also know just how valuable it would be to have someone come alongside and reaffirm the righteous behavior that has prompted the persecution.

Do you have a friend suffering the backlash of someone else's scorn because of their faith in the Lord? More than just affirming the right things they do, why not affirm the right attitudes you see in them from our study of the Beatitudes? Is this person poor in spirit? Gentle? Merciful?

Use the space provided to prepare your thoughts for encouraging this person to persevere.

Poor in spirit: _____

_____

Mourning: _____

_____

Gentle: _____

_____

Hunger and thirst for righteousness: _____

_____

Merciful: _____

_____

Pure in heart: _____

_____

Peacemaker: _____

_____

Persecuted: _____

_____

Chapter 12

THE INFLUENCE
OF A SERVANT

Matthew 5:13–16

Servants who are poor in spirit, gentle, merciful, and pure in heart are wonderful to behold . . . but are they practical? What possible down-to-earth influence can they have in the kind of depraved and dark world the apostle Paul describes in 2 Timothy 3?

> But realize this, that in the last days difficult times will come. For men will be lovers of self, lovers of money, boastful, arrogant, revilers, disobedient to parents, ungrateful, unholy, unloving, irreconcilable, malicious gossips, without self-control, brutal, haters of good, treacherous, reckless, conceited, lovers of pleasure rather than lovers of God; holding to a form of godliness, although they have denied its power; and avoid such men as these. For among them are those who enter into households and captivate weak women weighed down with sins, led on by various impulses, always learning and never able to come to the knowledge of the truth. (vv. 1–7)

That's our world, the real world—"difficult times." And a humble servant is going to impact such a violent and dangerous place? How? In what way?

Indispensable Influences for Good

Immediately after the Beatitudes in Matthew 5, Jesus describes two unique ways the life of a servant affects the world for good.

"The Salt of the Earth"

You may remember that throughout the Beatitudes Jesus repeatedly used the plural "they." Blessed are "those" . . . for "they" shall inherit, for "theirs" is the kingdom, for "they" shall be comforted. Now, in verse 13, He uses the more pointed "you" to introduce the servant's role as a preservative in a decaying world.

"You are the salt of the earth." (v. 13a)

According to Stuart Briscoe, Jesus' closest listeners, the fishermen of Galilee, immediately understood the message behind the metaphor. He writes,

> For them, salt was not something in a shiny silver shaker on the dinner table. It was a preservative, vital to their way of life. Once they caught a fish, they had to get it to market. The only way to get it there in marketable condition was to salt it down. . . . Salt arrested corruption; it kept fish fresh and edible.[1]

The world was once fresh, a perfect and unspoiled garden of delights. Sin contaminated that creation, however, and its corrupting influence causes the "difficult times"—the moral decay and rotting selfishness we see around us every day. That's why unsaved humanity is consistently described throughout the New Testament as "perishing" (see 1 Cor. 1:18a; 2 Cor. 2:15; 4:3).

The presence of true servants in this dying world acts as a preserving agent to arrest corruption. Our mercy, gentleness, and purity in heart restrain godlessness from spreading; but they do much more than that.

Salt also creates a thirst. A servant's unselfish lifestyle can cause others who are perishing to thirst for Christ's living water (see John 7:37–38).

Yet another purpose of salt is to add flavor. William Barclay translates this truth into the Christian servant's life.

> Food without salt is a sadly insipid and even a sickening thing. Christianity is to life what salt is to food. Christianity lends flavour to life.
>
> The tragedy is that so often people have connected Christianity with precisely the opposite. They have connected Christianity with that which takes the flavour out of life. . . .
>
> . . . There should be a sheer sparkle about the Christian but too often he dresses like a mourner at

---

1. Stuart Briscoe, *Now for Something Totally Different: A Study of the Sermon on the Mount* (Waco, Tex.: Word Books Publisher, 1978), pp. 51–52.

a funeral, and talks like a spectre at a feast. Wherever he is, if he is to be the salt of the earth, the Christian must be the diffuser of joy.[2]

To preserve, create thirst, and add flavor—these are all wonderful ways the servant can salt the world for good. "But," Jesus goes on to warn,

> "if the salt has become tasteless, how will it be made salty again? It is good for nothing anymore, except to be thrown out and trampled under foot by men." (Matt. 5:13b)

A servant's saltiness comes from exemplifying the very qualities Jesus outlined in the Beatitudes. The more pure in character we become, the stronger our influence. The more we contaminate ourselves with the impurities of worldly attitudes and actions, the less influence and use we will have as salt.

One final thought about salt before we go on: Always remember that salt is shaken, not poured. In other words, spread yourself out so that you're touching the lives of non-Christians; don't simply pour yourself into the church and other church-related activities. Christians who clump together with other believers, never reaching out into society, tend to become petty and distasteful. Spread yourself around—with the unsaved at work, in the neighborhood, at that volunteer organization, in all endeavors—salt the earth!

"The Light of the World"

Again, using the arresting *you*, Jesus introduces a second illustration, beginning with verse 14.

> "You are the light of the world. A city set on a hill cannot be hidden. Nor do men light a lamp, and put it under the peck-measure, but on the lampstand; and it gives light to all who are in the house." (vv. 14–15)

The basic function of light is to dispel darkness. In the same way, Christians are to dispel the darkness by reflecting the radiance of Christ.

---

2. William Barclay, *The Gospel of Matthew*, vol. 1, rev. ed., The Daily Study Bible Series (Philadelphia, Pa.: Westminster Press, 1975), pp. 120–21. Used by kind permission of The Saint Andrew Press, Edinburgh, Scotland.

Now, in order for that to happen, our Christlike character can't be hidden or limited. Rather, as Jesus goes on to say,

> "Let your light shine before men in such a way that they may see your good works, and glorify your Father who is in heaven." (v. 16)

With an enlightening pen, Barclay writes:

> Christianity is something which is meant to be seen. As someone has well said, "There can be no such thing as secret discipleship, for either the secrecy destroys the discipleship, or the discipleship destroys the secrecy. . . ."
>
> . . . Our Christianity should be visible in the way we treat a shop assistant across the counter, in the way we order a meal in a restaurant, in the way we treat our employees or serve our employer, in the way we play a game or drive or park a motor car, in the daily language we use, in the literature we read. A Christian should be just as much a Christian in the factory, the workshop, the shipyard, the mine, the schoolroom, the surgery, the kitchen, the golf course, the playing field as he is in church.[3]

The brightness with which we shine as lights depends on the quality of our good works. Not on our words, necessarily, for light is silent. If you reflect the kind of good works Jesus has outlined for us in the Beatitudes, few words will be necessary in order for others to see Him and glorify our Father.

Remember, too, that light gives direction. In the light of a Christian's example, others are able to see the way to Christ. Sin is exposed, truth is revealed, and the narrow way to life is found.

Still another function of light is to attract attention. Be assured that living like Christ will draw the attention of those around you who are walking in darkness. They cannot help but notice the light that suddenly pierces the night each time they are around you. Like moths, they will be irresistibly drawn, some to salvation and life, some to a searing rejection of that light and death.

---

3. Barclay, *The Gospel of Matthew*, p. 123.

Personal Response to Our Role

Our influence and its outcome is sobering. Jesus has privileged us with an incredible ability to impact others for good. So what is the right response to such a role?

First, *remember that you are different*. Our uniqueness from the world should be as noticeable as salt is from decay and light is from darkness. Unfortunately, as John Stott reminds us, this great strength of ours is often our greatest weakness. He writes,

> Probably the greatest tragedy of the church through-out its long and chequered history has been its constant tendency to conform to the prevailing culture instead of developing a Christian counter-culture.[4]

Second, *commit to being responsible*. Each of us has a responsibility not only to be salt but also to keep from being contaminated. And we have a responsibility not only to be light but to allow His light to shine brightly.

Third, and last, *never forget that you are influential*. Never doubt the impact of even the smallest good work you may perform. Every Christian is influential; and with God accomplishing His works through ours, who can say what great things He will do with your life! If you doubt that, just remember what He did with that handful of Palestinian peasants He called His disciples.

Living Insights

"Christians are to be 'rubbed' into culture," Charles Colson writes in *The Body*, not "so busy building visible institutions— buildings and retreat centers and places for fellowship—that we are in danger of becoming pillars of salt."[5]

Colson goes on to relate a favorite story of how one man managed to rub his Christian influence into one of life's darkest places—our prisons.

4. John R. W. Stott, *The Message of the Sermon on the Mount (Matthew 5–7): Christian Counter-Culture* (Downers Grove, Ill.: InterVarsity Press, 1978), p. 63.

5. Charles Colson, with Ellen Santilli Vaughn, *The Body: Being Light in Darkness* (Dallas, Tex.: Word Publishing, 1992), p. 366.

In 1984, when North Carolina Governor James Martin asked Aaron Johnson to join his state government team, he said that he wanted this Secretary of Correction to be different from all the rest. Governor Martin got what he was looking for.

Aaron Johnson was the first black to be appointed to the position in North Carolina—and the only ordained minister in the nation to hold such a job. And from his first day in office, he made God's presence felt.

When he arrived in Raleigh in January 1985, Aaron Johnson walked into his large, gracious office, stared at the huge desk, the official insignia, the trappings of power, and dropped to his knees. *Lord,* he prayed, *here I am. Use me however You want to.* Then he got up and called in his chief legal adviser.

"Tell me," said Johnson, "how much power does a secretary of correction have?"

"As much as you want," responded his aide.

"I mean from a statutory standpoint, how much authority do I have?"

The adviser looked him in the eye. "Mr. Secretary," he said, "you can do what you want in these prisons."

"Well, then," responded Johnson, "I want to stop the cursing in them, taking the Lord's name in vain. The profanity in these places is horrible."

"Are you serious, Mr. Secretary?" the aide stammered.

"I am dead serious. I want the very first order I send out to be an anti-cursing ordinance. You find a way to do it."

The aide left, shaking his head. He returned a few hours later, dust from old law books covering his sleeves. "I found it, Mr. Secretary!" he said. "There's a statute against cursing in public—and we can use it to issue your order!"

And thus profanity was prohibited within the North Carolina prison system.

Soon after that, Aaron Johnson discovered that soft-core pornography magazines were being bought at state expense for inmates. He called in his legal counsel.

"How much authority do I have?" he asked.

By now the adviser was ready for anything. "What do you want to do?" he asked.

"I want to stop *Playboy* magazines from coming into the prisons," said Johnson. "Can I do that?"

"You're the secretary!" responded the aide.

And so, by official order, *Playboy* magazines were barred from North Carolina prisons.

Now this doesn't mean that never a foul word nor a lascivious thought exits the mouths or enters the minds of North Carolina inmates. But it does show that a Christian can be a direct, righteous influence on his or her environment.[6]

We all love stories like this. But many of us walk away from them unchanged in our thinking because our lives are so different from Johnson's. As Colson writes, very few of us are

placed in a position of authority where we can issue an order and fifteen thousand employees and twenty thousand prisoners will have to obey us. But all of us can be—*must* be—salt wherever we find ourselves. . . .

And we begin, like Aaron Johnson, by falling on our knees in our workplace, our kitchen, our classroom, our neighborhood and praying those simple words, "Lord, here I am. Use me however You want to."[7]

Will you make this your prayer concerning the spheres of influence God has given you? If you do, follow it up with some time spent brainstorming different ways you might spread the salt of Christ's presence in each place.

Brainstorming

_____   _____

6. Colson, *The Body*, pp. 368–69.
7. Colson, *The Body*, pp. 378, 379.

_____   _____

_____   _____

_____   _____

_____   _____

🍵 *Living Insights* STUDY TWO

In *The Body,* Chuck Colson concludes a chapter titled "Being the Salt" with an important insight many Christians fail to see or understand. He writes:

> **Each of us must see ourselves as ministers of the gospel.** We don't simply attend church, consuming a religious product. Rather, our whole understanding of ourselves as members of the Body is directed toward being equipped to serve effectively in our vocation and our community—wherever God places us.
>
> Many Christians have a bifurcated view of life: Faith is over here in this compartment, and the rest of life—work, family, leisure time, and everything else—is over there.
>
> Like the young woman who stopped me in an airport recently, "Mr. Colson, I so admire the work that Prison Fellowship is doing. I'm a believer; I wish that I could be in full-time Christian service like you."
>
> "What is it you do?" I asked.
>
> "Well, I'm still in school," she said. "I'm finishing up my doctoral work in molecular biology. I had planned to teach full time. I love it. But lately I've realized I should do more for the Lord. My parents were missionaries. I'm thinking of going to Brazil as a missionary."
>
> "You are in a tremendous position to be a missionary right where you are!" I said adamantly. "How many Christians are there who are molecular biologists? The university needs people like you!"

She looked relieved, even excited, as it sank in: She was a missionary right where she was.

There are thousands of Christians who suffer from this same kind of false understanding of the glory of vocation, and a parallel misunderstanding of how God places particular people in particular places in every arena to be salt and accomplish His preserving, flavoring purposes.[8]

Could you be one of those thousands? Have you bought into the lie that says to be involved in ministry you must earn a theological degree and wear a clerical collar? Friend, you are salt and light; you already are a missionary, an ambassador for Christ wherever you go, whatever you do. Don't abandon the privilege and opportunities God has given you right where you are to impact those around you for Christ.

8. Colson, *The Body*, p. 378.

Chapter 13
THE PERILS OF A SERVANT
2 Kings 4–5

Every calling, every occupation, every position has its own peculiar perils. Steeplejacks hang from incredible heights, undercover cops gamble their lives on dangerous deceptions, and AIDS researchers risk infection from the very disease they're trying to cure. Everyone can easily perceive the perils in these and many other jobs. But who would ever think that being a servant could be perilous too?

It is more dangerous, perhaps, than most of us realize. And this is due, in part, to some misconceptions that leave us blindly vulnerable to the perils of servanthood.

Some Common Misconceptions

To avoid some of these perils, we must first let the winds of Scripture clear away our foggy ideas, one at a time.

Misconception #1: Servants Have Special Powers in Themselves

Often, young and immature Christians tend to put spiritual mentors and popular preachers on pedestals. They look upon them as having some angelic anointing that endows them with supernatural abilities. It was this same naive thinking that blinded Jim Jones' followers and ultimately led them to commit mass suicide in a South American jungle.

The apostle Paul, however, makes it clear that servants possess no special powers in and of themselves:

> Not that we are adequate in ourselves to consider anything as coming from ourselves, but our adequacy is from God, who also made us adequate as servants. (2 Cor. 3:5–6a)

Misconception #2: Servants Don't Struggle with Everyday Problems

Implanted in some people's minds is the idea that the more holy and selfless you become, the less you struggle with life's problems.

Servanthood is seen as a sort of spiritual staircase that leads its devotees up out of affliction and onto higher planes of prosperity. Not true, says Paul.

> We are afflicted in every way, but not crushed; perplexed, but not despairing; persecuted, but not forsaken; struck down, but not destroyed. (4:8–9)

Problems? Paul had plenty of them. Just look at the terms he used to describe them. *Afflicted*—the word literally means "to press." It refers to being squeezed by the pressure of difficult circumstances or antagonistic people. *Perplexed*—the Greek word is a combination of two terms that mean "without a way," conveying the idea of feeling lost, not knowing which way to turn. *Persecuted*—this carries the picture of being pursued, put to flight with threats, being physically driven away by enemies. *Struck down*—to experience this is to be shoved down, pushed aside, or run over.

Misconception #3: Servants Are Protected against Subtle Dangers

The logic behind this thinking goes something like this: great servants aren't vulnerable to the petty perils of ordinary people. Big dangers, perhaps—everyone is susceptible to those. But small, innocuous-looking dangers? Spiritual giants can stride right over them.

But in light of the problems we just examined, listen to the way Paul describes his life:

> Always carrying about in the body the dying of Jesus, that the life of Jesus also may be manifested in our body. For we who live are constantly being delivered over to death for Jesus' sake, that the life of Jesus also may be manifested in our mortal flesh. (vv. 10–11)

The key phrase, "constantly being delivered over to death," according to commentator Murray J. Harris, means that Paul

> faced perilous hazards every hour and death every day. . . .
> Both verses stress . . . the fact that the death and the life of Jesus were simultaneously evident in the apostle's experience (cf. 1:4, 5). It was not a matter of life after death, or even of life through

death, but of life in the midst of death.[1]

Though not explicitly expressed, it is clear from the Apostle's experience that being a servant in no way protected him from dangers—no matter how overt or subtle they were. And oftentimes, it is not the easily recognizable dangers that pose the greatest threat to servants. Subtle dangers, like the ones we shall see in the life of a servant named Gehazi, are often the most deadly.

A Case Study: Gehazi, the Servant of Elisha

Gehazi was the rather obscure servant of one of Israel's great prophets—Elisha. The lessons we can learn from Gehazi's service, however, are anything but obscure. So let's begin by journeying back to the Old Testament to acquaint ourselves with his story.

Background and Role

As we step into the world of 2 Kings, we find ourselves in a time of chaos and corruption in Israel. For generations, one wicked ruler after another has occupied the nation's throne, leading the citizens to great depths of depravity. To rescue His people from their downward descent, the Lord had raised up the prophet Elijah. At the end of his courageous service, as he was whisked into heaven on a whirlwind, the mantle of prophetic power and position fell to Elisha (see 2 Kings 2:8–14).

Picking up Elisha's story a little further on in chapter 4, we find the prophet being thoughtfully cared for by a Shunammite woman and her husband—who go so far as to build an extra room onto their home just for Elisha's visits (vv. 8–10). And it is here, in this comfortable setting, that we first meet Gehazi (v. 12).

Our first glimpse of him is a favorable one. The Shunammite woman has been gracious in her hospitality toward Elisha, but the prophet is unsure of how to repay her kindness (vv. 11–14a). So Gehazi sensitively suggests that he make it possible for her to conceive a son, pointing out that she is childless—which was considered a great tragedy in that day—and that she will probably remain so because of her husband's age (v. 14b).

The gift is granted, as we read in verses 15–17, and the child

---

1. Murray J. Harris, "2 Corinthians," in *The Expositor's Bible Commentary*, ed. Frank E. Gaebelein (Grand Rapids, Mich.: Zondervan Publishing House, Regency Reference Library, 1976), pp. 342–43.

grows to become a young lad. One day, however, as he is with his father in the harvest fields, he suddenly has great pains in his head. He is immediately taken home, only to die soon after in his mother's arms (vv. 18–20). Naturally, the Shunammite woman thinks of Elisha and promptly sets out to find the prophet—and, hopefully, a second miracle that will return to her the precious gift that has been taken (vv. 21–24).

Temptations and Reactions

Now we come to that time in Gehazi's service when he faces four perils common to all servants who work alongside gifted leaders.

First: *The peril of overprotection and possessiveness.* Notice, first of all, Gehazi's reaction when the desperate mother approaches the prophet.

> When she came to the man of God to the hill, she caught hold of his feet. And Gehazi came near to push her away; but the man of God said, "Let her alone, for her soul is troubled within her; and the Lord has hidden it from me and has not told me." Then she said, "Did I ask for a son from my lord? Did I not say, 'Do not deceive me'?" (vv. 27–28)

Gehazi is commendably committed to protect Elisha, but isn't it strange that he would treat the woman roughly after having been so sensitive to her plight earlier? That happens sometimes to those who jealously seek to protect the ones they serve. They can easily become so overprotective and possessive that they miss seeing the needs of others (see also Num. 11:24–30).

Second: *The peril of feeling used and unappreciated.* Unfortunately for Gehazi, things only go from bad to worse. Elisha is moved with compassion for this woman and immediately devises a plan to bring her son back to life. Handing Gehazi his staff, Elisha tells him to run to the woman's house, disregarding anyone who would hinder his mission. Once there, he is to lay the staff on the boy's face. So off Gehazi goes, following the instruction perfectly . . . but nothing happens (2 Kings 4: 29–31). Things change quickly, however, when his master arrives and takes control.

> When Elisha came into the house, behold the lad was dead and laid on his bed. So he entered and shut the door behind them both, and prayed to the

110

Lord. And he went up and lay on the child, and put his mouth on his mouth and his eyes on his eyes and his hands on his hands, and he stretched himself on him; and the flesh of the child became warm. Then he returned and walked in the house once back and forth, and went up and stretched himself on him; and the lad sneezed seven times and the lad opened his eyes. And he called Gehazi and said, "Call this Shunammite." So he called her. And when she came in to him, he said, "Take up your son." Then she went in and fell at his feet and bowed herself to the ground, and she took up her son and went out. (vv. 32–37)

It must have been an incredible moment for the mother. Certainly a gratifying experience for Elisha. But for Gehazi? A perilous time of temptation.

Try to identify with some of the very human thoughts and feelings Gehazi probably had as he watched the Shunammite woman lavishly honor Elisha for reviving her son. Wouldn't you suspect he was feeling a little humiliated about his aborted effort? He had done all that Elisha had told him, so why didn't it work? Elisha shouldn't have sent him on a fool's errand if he was just going to come and perform the miracle himself anyway.

Thoughts like these can plant in a servant's heart subtle seeds of discontent that will blossom into feelings of being used and unappreciated. All those who serve others will eventually feel the presence, real or imagined, of this particular peril. Gehazi's seeds get a chance to root even more deeply in the next unhappy incident.

Elisha tells Gehazi to make a stew for some prophets who are visiting him in Gilgal, so he goes out and gathers some herbs and wild gourds that catch his eye (vv. 38–40a). As the aromatic entrée is dished out and the first bites are taken, the prophets suddenly cry out,

"O man of God, there is death in the pot." And they were unable to eat. But [Elisha] said, "Now bring meal." And he threw it into the pot, and he said, "Pour it out for the people that they may eat." Then there was no harm in the pot. (vv. 40b–41)

Once again Gehazi is probably feeling like he flubbed up, and once again it is Elisha who comes in and miraculously saves the day. While everyone else is singing Elisha's praises, Gehazi may well have been wondering, When will I get to do things right and be appreciated?

Moving ahead to chapter 5, an entirely different experience awaits Gehazi, bringing with it two more hidden perils, the latter of which finally entraps him.

Third: *The peril of experiencing undeserved disrespect and resentment.* It all begins with the introduction of a high-ranking Syrian soldier.

> Now Naaman, captain of the army of the king of Aram, was a great man with his master, and highly respected, because by him the Lord had given victory to Aram. The man was also a valiant warrior, but he was a leper. (v. 1)

Naaman has clout, courage, and the command of the king's army—but he also has leprosy. And that is his greatest enemy, one he can't defeat in battle. So, through a series of events (vv. 1–8), the officer is led to Elisha for cleansing from this foe.

> So Naaman came with his horses and his chariots, and stood at the doorway of the house of Elisha. And Elisha sent a messenger to him, saying, "Go and wash in the Jordan seven times, and your flesh shall be restored to you and you shall be clean." But Naaman was furious and went away and said, "Behold, I thought, 'He will surely come out to me, and stand and call on the name of the Lord his God, and wave his hand over the place, and cure the leper.' Are not Abanah and Pharpar, the rivers of Damascus, better than all the waters of Israel? Could I not wash in them and be clean?" (vv. 9–12)

Naaman doesn't simply come to Elisha's home, he "arrives" with all the pomp and pageantry awarded someone of his status. But Elisha isn't the least bit impressed by all the horses and chariots and decides to send a messenger out to communicate the cure. And who do you think it probably is? The text doesn't say, but very likely it could be our friend Gehazi.

Now picture the situation. Gehazi isn't the prophet, but he has to speak the prophet's words to a proud warrior who isn't going to appreciate the message or the messenger. And he doesn't. Naaman becomes furious, ranting and raving at Gehazi, who bears the full brunt of his rage. Finally, the Syrian officer storms off, leaving behind a very frazzled servant sorely tested by a third temptation: having to speak the truth to those who won't like what they hear.

All servants will occasionally find themselves in Gehazi's shoes. Today, the truth we give will not be that of a prophet but of the Lord from His Word. And regardless of how graciously the truth is communicated, a servant is likely to be caught in a painful cross fire of resentment and rejection.[2]

The good news of Naaman's story, however, is that he does finally calm down and follow Elisha's instructions. In gratitude for his miraculous healing, the Syrian officer returns to offer Elisha a sizable gift. Don't forget that it was Gehazi who told Naaman what to do and suffered his abuse, but now it is Elisha who is offered a reward. The prophet honorably refuses the offer and sends Naaman on his way in peace. Gehazi, unfortunately, cannot resist that reward, and it lures him into a snare that will cost him dearly.

Fourth: *The peril of hidden greed.* This is the secret, smoldering desire to be rewarded, applauded, and exalted. Gehazi's greed was sparked by Naaman's offer and now quickly rages out of control. "If Elisha won't help himself to the reward, I will!" Gehazi thinks, and he literally runs to stake his claim with Naaman.

> When Naaman saw one running after him, he came down from the chariot to meet him and said, "Is all well?" And he said, "All is well. My master has sent me, saying, 'Behold, just now two young men of the sons of the prophets have come to me from the hill country of Ephraim. Please give them a talent of silver and two changes of clothes.'" And Naaman said, "Be pleased to take two talents." And he urged him, and bound two talents of silver in two bags with two changes of clothes, and gave them to two of his servants; and they carried them before him. When he came to the hill, he took them from their hand and deposited them in the house, and he sent the men away, and they departed. (vv. 21b–24)

2. For further study on how servants are to approach others with the truth, read Galatians 6:1 and 2 Timothy 2:24–26.

Exposure and Judgment

Gehazi doesn't have long to enjoy the bounty gained by his greed. No sooner has he hidden it all away than his master confronts him: "Where have you been, Gehazi?" And he smoothly lies, "Your servant went nowhere" (v. 25b). With that, Gehazi seals his fate. He has sold out his servanthood for two talents of silver and two changes of clothes. Elisha exposes his deception and pronounces the terrible price he and his descendants shall have to pay.

> "Did not my heart go with you, when the man turned from his chariot to meet you? Is it a time to receive money and to receive clothes and olive groves and vineyards and sheep and oxen and male and female servants? Therefore, the leprosy of Naaman shall cleave to you and to your descendants forever." So he went out from his presence a leper as white as snow. (vv. 26–27)

Some Lingering Lessons

Gehazi's life is a sobering reminder that even servanthood has its perils. So to help safeguard against the dangers he faced, which are common to us all, here are three lessons to remember. First, *no servant is completely safe.* If you think being a servant protects you from peril, you set yourself up to become easily ensnared. Second, *most actions will be unrewarded initially.* It helps to know this, especially if you need a lot of affirmation to stay committed to something. More often than not, the only reward servants receive now comes from a sense of satisfaction that God gives for following Him. And, third, *all motives must be honestly examined.* You must learn to ask yourself, Why am I doing this? before you jump into something. Learn from Gehazi—check your motives.

🍵 *Living Insights* STUDY ONE

Greed is so subtle. It's a chameleon that blends into our thinking so that it's next to impossible to detect. Asceticism cannot kill it. Materialism cannot pacify it. And being a servant cannot protect us from it.

Worse still, servanthood is a high-risk role for this particular peril. Why? Because greed thrives on discontent. And it is oh-so-easy to become discontented when selflessly serving others. For example:

- When you do the work and somebody else gets the praise

- When you feel used and unappreciated

- When you receive undeserved disrespect and resentment

Gehazi could have easily felt discontented over any of those situations and started craving Elisha's prestige and power. Instead, he became dissatisfied when Elisha turned down Naaman's reward. Perhaps it was because he compared his humble possessions with the riches offered by the Syrian officer. And that was all it took to stir up some "I-deserve-better-than-this" kinds of feelings that powerfully drove him to succumb to greed.

Have you ever done that—compared yourself to someone else? Of course you have; we all do. And comparison is one of the quickest downhill slides to discontent and greed any of us can travel.

Maybe you're feeling discontented right now. Is it because you're comparing yourself, your bank account, or your popularity with somebody else's? Can you think of any specific areas?

_____

_____

_____

To weed out the discontent that breeds greed, we must stop comparing. It's that simple . . . at least, saying it is simple, but it is tremendously difficult to do! Part of the solution is exercising the mental discipline to stop all comparisons. Try it; ask God for His help in sensitizing you to this particular problem so that you can weed it out. You'll probably be amazed at how much time and energy you've been spending comparing yourself to others.

📖 *Living Insights* STUDY TWO

Let's expand our thinking about the four perils a servant may face by identifying other biblical characters who faced them as well. For example:

1. *Peril of overprotection and possessiveness:* Peter and the rest of the disciples in Mark 8:31–33; 10:13–14; Luke 18:35–43.

2. *Peril of feeling used and unappreciated:* Moses in Numbers 11:1–15; Elijah in 1 Kings 19:1–4.

3. *Peril of undeserved disrespect and resentment:* Samuel in 1 Samuel 8:4–8; David in 25:2–11a.

4. *Peril of hidden greed:* Ananias and Sapphira in Acts 4:32–5:10; Simon in 8:9–20.

Can you think of some positive examples of people who resisted the downward pull of these perils?

_____   _____

_____   _____

_____   _____

Have any of these examples helped remind you of a particular peril in your life? Is there an insight from the positive examples that might help you with a peril you are facing?

Chapter 14

THE OBEDIENCE
OF A SERVANT
John 13:12–17

If you were to describe yourself with just two words, what would they be?

Powerful and *dynamic?*

Warm and *winsome?*

Gifted and *visionary?*

How about *gentle* and *humble?* OK, OK, it was just a suggestion. Not a very appealing one, though, right? Probably for many of us, these two words didn't even enter our minds as an option. But if they had, it's likely we would've promptly rejected them for sounding too passive and unimpressive. And yet, ironically, they are the very words the greatest individual to ever live used to describe Himself.

Self-Description of Jesus Christ

> "Take My yoke upon you, and learn from Me, for I
> am gentle and humble in heart; and you shall find
> rest for your souls." (Matt. 11:29)

You would expect someone like Jesus, whose life is the center-piece of history, to describe Himself with such exalted words as *all-powerful* and *all-knowing*, not *gentle* and *humble*. But these two un-likely words are the blueprint to His character, which He wants us to use as a pattern for our own lives.

Let's take a moment to look closely at the personality those two words construct. The Greek term Matthew uses for "gentle," *praus*, speaks of strength under control. As we saw in chapter 10, it's used of a wild stallion that's been tamed. The horse is still strong, still muscular, but under control. And you'll probably also recall that this same word is used of a soothing ointment that takes the sting out of a wound. That's one dimension of the Savior's character.

The second word Jesus mentions, "humble," comes from the Greek term *tapeinos*, which means "to be made low." According to the *Theological Dictionary of the New Testament*, it refers to "the small and insignificant services by which one can help the other."[1] Basically, it is a servant word, one that has unselfishness and thoughtfulness mixed in with it.

Together, the qualities of gentleness and humility form the unusual image of the most powerful life ever lived. And it is that same image that the Father is committed to forming in each of us (see Rom. 8:28–29).

Illustration of That Description

Because it is so much more helpful to see something rather than just describe it, let's turn to John 13, where we'll find one of the most indelible images of Jesus' gentleness and humility in all of Scripture.

Background Information

The scene that unfolds in John 13 is set in the borrowed guest room of a first-century home in Jerusalem. In that day of dirt paths and dusty streets, it was customary for a host to station a servant at the door to wash the feet of the guests as they arrived. On those occasions when there was no servant, someone would often volunteer to fulfill that role. Yet when the disciples gathered in the Upper Room with Jesus to celebrate Passover, not one of them volunteered. It seems that Peter, John, Matthew, and the rest were too busy arguing about which of them would be the greatest in Christ's kingdom (see Luke 22:24–30).

Imagine Jesus' disappointment. For three years He has taught and modeled servanthood to these men, and they still haven't caught on to the concept. Now the horrific hour of His arrest and crucifixion is about to overtake Him. What can He do in the little time left? Ah, there's a basin and a towel . . .

Personal Demonstration

> [Jesus] rose from supper, and laid aside His garments; and taking a towel, He girded Himself about. Then He poured water into the basin, and began to wash the disciples' feet, and to wipe them with the towel with which He was girded. And so He came to Simon

---

1. Gerhard Friedrich, ed., *Theological Dictionary of the New Testament*, trans. and ed. Geoffrey W. Bromiley (Grand Rapids, Mich.: William B. Eerdmans Publishing Co., 1972), vol. 8, p. 20.

Peter. He said to Him, "Lord, do You wash my feet?"
Jesus answered and said to him, "What I do you do
not realize now, but you shall understand hereafter."
Peter said to Him, "Never shall You wash my feet!"
Jesus answered him, "If I do not wash you, you have
no part with Me." Simon Peter said to Him, "Lord,
not my feet only, but also my hands and my head."
Jesus said to him, "He who has bathed needs only
to wash his feet, but is completely clean; and you
are clean, but not all of you." (John 13:4–10)

The dust of two thousand years has not obscured the power of
that one act of servanthood or the lessons we can learn from it. For
example, when Jesus rose from the table, He didn't say, "I am now
going to demonstrate humility." He just got up, grabbed the towel
and basin, and started quietly washing. True servanthood is like
that—*unannounced*. It doesn't draw attention to itself with loud
proclamations and gaudy displays like the Pharisees used to do.
"They do all their deeds to be noticed by men," Jesus had warned
His disciples.

> "For they broaden their phylacteries, and lengthen the
> tassels of their garments. And they love the place of
> honor at banquets, and the chief seats in the syna-
> gogues, and respectful greetings in the market places,
> and being called by men, Rabbi. . . . But the great-
> est among you shall be your servant. And whoever
> exalts himself shall be humbled; and whoever hum-
> bles himself shall be exalted." (Matt. 23:5–7, 11–12)

True servanthood is also *as willing to receive as to give*. Notice
Peter's pronouncement when Jesus approached him with the basin?
"Never shall You wash my feet!" (John 13:8a). For that outspoken
fisherman, the thought of Christ serving him was absolutely out of
the question. But why? Was it because his pride got in the way?
Was it too humbling for him to have the Lord wiping his feet?
Perhaps, if the truth were known, many of us are also much more
comfortable giving than receiving. Receiving means admitting we
have a need, and that rubs our pride the wrong way.

In his book *The Frog Who Never Became a Prince*, James "Frog"
Sullivan writes of the struggle he went through to learn how to
receive as well as give.

The thing that destroys a good many of us as Christians is our inability to relate to each other in a warm, honest, compassionate sort of way. Even with those to whom I was close, I failed in this endeavor. I was so busy being a "doing" Christian (Boy, that certainly was me!) that I'd forgotten what God called me to *be*. For so long I didn't know that a Christian was supposed to let someone love him; I thought that he was always supposed to be loving somebody else. I didn't think it was necessary to let anyone love me, including [my wife] Carolyn. It seems that in the context of my Christian faith, you were adequate if you could love people; but you were considered inadequate if you let them love you.

Great things began to happen in my life when I found out how much I needed love from Carolyn and my children. I came to terms with how much I needed other Christians around me. . . . I began to realize that God is the one who gives; and we are the ones who receive. I discovered giving love is not difficult for some of us; but for me, receiving love and letting people love me was one of the most trying things that I as a Christian had to learn.[2]

We can also learn from Jesus' example that *being a servant is not a sign of weakness but of incredible strength*. Jesus didn't hesitate to throw down the gauntlet to Peter—if He didn't wash his feet, they were through! This was hardly the resolve of a weak and spineless person. Only someone with tremendous inner strength would have the courage to confront a close friend like that. And in the presence of that strength, Peter's unbridled boldness was brought under control: "Lord, not my feet only, but also my hands and my head" (v. 9).

Direct Admonition

When Christ finished washing the disciples' feet, the Scriptures say that He reclined at the table again and asked, "Do you know what I have done to you?" (v. 12). Can you imagine how strange that question must have sounded to the disciples? Of course they

2. James "Frog" Sullivan, *The Frog Who Never Became a Prince* (Santa Ana, Calif.: Vision House Publishers, 1975), pp. 130–31.

knew; He washed their feet. But Jesus' question wasn't as simplistic as it sounds. He was trying to get them to look below the surface. So He continued,

> "You call Me Teacher and Lord; and you are right, for so I am. If I then, the Lord and the Teacher, washed your feet, . . ." (vv. 13–14a)

". . . then, in turn, we should be willing to wash Your feet" is probably what the disciples thought he was going to say. That would seem the obvious and expected lesson Jesus was getting at. But Christ surprised them with a different conclusion:

> ". . . you also ought to wash one another's feet." (v. 14b)

If Jesus had asked any one of the disciples to get up and wash His feet, that person would have gladly done so. We all would have been honored to. But would we be just as eager to wash our neighbor's feet or the feet of those who are sick or hurting or needy? That's servanthood. That's the example Jesus wants us to follow.

> "For I gave you an example that you also should do as I did to you. Truly, truly, I say to you, a slave is not greater than his master; neither is one who is sent greater than the one who sent him. If you know these things, you are blessed if you do them." (vv. 15–17)

What is it that we're to do with Jesus' model? Study it on Sunday mornings? Discuss it in a group? Memorize it so we can be sure to quote it accurately? No, He gave us His example so that we would imitate it, put it into practice in our own lives. And to do that calls for obedience. That's the response He expects from us—"Do as I did to you."

Appropriation of Christ's Admonition

As we each seek to follow Christ's example, we need to remember three keys to obedience.

First, *obedience means personal involvement*. We can't wash someone's feet at a distance or indirectly or *in absentia*. Nor do we wash feet simply by reading about someone who did. Servanthood requires that we stoop, that we get wet, that we get involved in meeting the needs of others in a personal way.

Second, *obedience requires Christlike unselfishness.* Oftentimes, we hesitate to serve, not because we don't know how, but because to do so would mean risking, stepping out of our comfort zones, giving up our preferences for His. Are we willing to do that?

Third, *obedience results in ultimate happiness.* The joy of serving is reserved for only those who actually roll up their sleeves and wash a few feet. It won't happen just by theorizing about serving; we've got to get involved in the same gentle and humble way Jesus did.

▮🍵 *Living Insights* — STUDY ONE

Some of us can be pretty rough in the way we wash other people's feet. We use scalding words like, "Give me that, genius, before you mess things up even worse" or, "Here, I'll do it myself. You're slower than molasses, you know that?" or, "You forgot to look, didn't you, dummy? Well, you've done a nice job of screwing this up. It'll take me all day to fix it."

Exaggerated, you think? Not really. Oh sure, we rarely speak that way to our neighbors in need; but when it's our son or daughter or parent or grandparent that needs a foot washing? Many of us take the skin off, we scrub so hard.

Why? How is it that we can pour ourselves out to gently wash the feet of the world, only to come home and treat the tender soles we find there with such harshness?

Is your attitude the proper temperature when you stoop to wash the feet in your family? Think back to the last time someone walked into your home with dirty feet. Did you respond with a gentle and humble attitude? Or were you boiling with anger and antagonism for being inconvenienced?

▮🍵 *Living Insights* — STUDY TWO

Foot washings were so common in Jesus' day. And yet, of all things, Jesus used this simple, lowly, unobtrusive act to challenge His disciples to become servants.

If it had been me, I probably would've chosen a more noticeable example—say, washing the feet of the five thousand with winged hands from heaven. But, no, Jesus just stuck with the simple, the ordinary. So why don't we? Instead of thinking we can't really serve because we can't sing like Amy Grant or preach like Billy Graham, why don't we look for those simple and unobtrusive ways of serving that are all around us? Think about it. Washing the disciples' feet was a very small thing, but consider the impact it had on them and on the world.

For the next few minutes or even for the rest of the day, try to discover as many simple ways as you can to wash the feet of those around you.

_____   _____

_____   _____

_____   _____

_____   _____

_____   _____

Chapter 15
OBEDIENCE PERSONIFIED
Genesis 22:1–19

Alan Redpath, in his biography of David, observed:

> The conversion of a soul is the miracle of a moment, the manufacture of a saint is the task of a lifetime.[1]

The apostle James referred to one of the most revered saints in all the Bible when he asked,

> Was not Abraham our father justified by works, when he offered up Isaac his son on the altar? (James 2:21)

This question contains the key to the manufacturing of Abraham from a callow convert into a serving saint: the test of obedience.

Time and again God put Abraham through the furnace of testing, each time with the plan of fashioning him into a stable servant of God, a man who would forever be known as "the friend of God" (v. 23).

Let's step back in time now, pausing to look at some of the first painful tests Abraham had to endure. Then we'll take a deep breath and climb the slopes of Mount Moriah to examine the worst crisis of obedience in that saintly patriarch's life.

Four Crises of Obedience in Abraham's Life

One thing we need to understand before we turn to these crises is the reason behind them. God did not put Abraham to the test to *see* if he was a believer, but to *show* the validity of his faith. James calls this being "justified by works" (v. 21), by which he means that Abraham proved himself to be a genuine servant by his works of obedience.

This chapter has been adapted from "Justified by Works," in the study guide *James: Practical and Authentic Living*, coauthored by Lee Hough, from the Bible-teaching ministry of Charles R. Swindoll (Fullerton, Calif.: Insight for Living, 1991).

1. Alan Redpath, *The Making of a Man of God* (Westwood, N.J.: Fleming H. Revell Co., 1962), p. 5.

Now, on to the tests themselves.

The first major crisis came when God told Abraham to leave his home (Gen. 12). At seventy-five, Abraham had to leave all that he knew and loved, everything that was familiar and dear to him, to set out for the unseen land of God's promise. Home disappeared behind him; a vast unknown stretched before him. But he obeyed God, said his good-byes, and willingly turned his back on Ur forever.

Abraham's second crisis occurred when he separated from his nephew Lot (Gen. 13). Though there was strife between Lot's herdsmen and his, Abraham nevertheless loved his nephew and cared about his welfare. But he also had the wisdom to do what he knew was best, so he separated from the young man and waited for God's next step.

The third major crisis came when God told Abraham to abandon his cherished plans for his first son, Ishmael (Gen. 17; see also 21:8–14). It was through Isaac, not the son of Sarah's handmaiden, that God wanted to rain down his blessings on Abraham. And though Abraham yearned for God's blessings, he still had a father's love for his firstborn. Can you not hear the ache in the old man's voice as he entreats the Lord?

> And Abraham said to God, "Oh that Ishmael might live before Thee!" (17:18)

But despite his fatherly love, Abraham determined to follow God's way and not his own.

Now we come to the fourth crisis, the greatest test of all. Abraham must be obedient to the God who has just asked him to sacrifice his beloved son—his only son now that Ishmael is gone—Isaac (Gen. 22).

Revelation of the Test

Let's turn to Genesis 22 and briefly investigate this final test of obedience. In doing so, we'll get a clearer picture of what is involved in being transformed into a serving saint of God.

> Now it came about after these things, that God tested Abraham, and said to him, "Abraham!" And he said, "Here I am." And He said, "Take now your son, your only son, whom you love, Isaac, and go to the land of Moriah; and offer him there as a burnt offering on one of the mountains of which I will tell you." (vv. 1–2)

125

The word *tested* in verse 1 is an intense form of the word in the original Hebrew. Used only here in the entire book of Genesis, it is actually saying that God *intensely* tested Abraham—that this was to be a test like no other.

By the way, there are times when God's tests are intense for us as well. Maybe you have just come through such an experience; perhaps that lies ahead for you. Wherever you are, there is hope in remembering this truth: God not only plans the length of our tests, He plans their depth as well. And He knows just how much we can endure (see Ps. 103:14).

Back in our Genesis passage, notice the progression God uses to reveal just who He wants sacrificed (v. 2). From this sequence, we are given a little window into the workings of Abraham's mind.

God: Take now your son.
Abraham: But I have two sons.
God: Your only son.
Abraham: Well, each is the only son of his mother.
God: Whom you love.
Abraham: Hmmm . . . I do love Ishmael.
God: ISAAC!
End of conversation.

To fully appreciate the emotional impact of this scene, you must remember that, by this time, Abraham was well over a hundred years old. He and Sarah had waited many years for the arrival of this son of promise, and it was only through him that God's blessings would come to fruition. How Abraham must have loved this child, and how he must have reeled to think of laying him on an altar as a burnt offering!

The Hebrew word used here for "offering," *'olah*, refers to a whole burnt offering, which would have included an animal's hooves, face, head, skin—*everything*. The entire animal would be consumed in smoke, and this is just what God has told Abraham to do with Isaac. A deep test indeed.[2]

---

2. "The 'burnt-offering,' (*'olah*), is the type of sacrifice best suited for this purpose, because it typifies complete surrender to God. The term is derived from the root *'alah*, signifying 'to go up,' i.e., in the smoke of the sacrifice. Therefore, the son given to Abraham is to be given back to Yahweh without reservations of any sort." H. C. Leupold, *Exposition of Genesis* (Grand Rapids, Mich.: Baker Book House, 1942), vol. 2, p. 621.

Response of Abraham

Verses 3–10 reveal four characteristics of Abraham's response, the first of which is found in verse 3.

> So Abraham rose early in the morning and saddled his donkey, and took two of his young men with him and Isaac his son; and he split wood for the burnt offering, and arose and went to the place of which God had told him.

Did you notice it? He *"rose early in the morning."* No procrastinating, no delays. Abraham's obedience was *immediate.*

How immediate are your responses to God? Do you sometimes find yourself stalling with that old standby, "I'll do it in a little while"? Keep in mind that one of Satan's most successful strategies is procrastination, getting us to drag our feet when we know we've had a clear command from God. Why not thwart the enemy of your soul by following Abraham's example instead?

Another aspect of Abraham's response was that it was *characterized by faith.*

> On the third day Abraham raised his eyes and saw the place from a distance. And Abraham said to his young men, "Stay here with the donkey, and I and the lad will go yonder; and we will worship and *return to you.*" (vv. 4–5, emphasis added)

What a remarkable statement! With the mountain of sacrifice looming in the distance, Abraham was able to focus on worshiping the Lord and trusting in His ability even to raise the dead if it came to that (see Heb. 11:19). And not one note of remorse, despondency, regret, or bitterness was sounded in all this symphony of obedient faithfulness.

Perhaps you've read this definition of faith: "Faith sees the invisible, believes the incredible, and receives the impossible."[3] It certainly applies to Abraham. He saw what couldn't be seen, believed in the unbelievable, and eagerly waited for God to achieve the impossible. He knew that impossibilities are God's specialty. Do you?

Leaving the servants behind, Abraham and Isaac began their slow ascent up Mount Moriah.

---

3. As quoted in *Encyclopedia of 7,700 Illustrations*, comp. Paul Lee Tan (Garland, Tex.: Bible Communications, Assurance Publishers, 1979), p. 405.

> And Abraham took the wood of the burnt offering and laid it on Isaac his son, and he took in his hand the fire and the knife. So the two of them walked on together. And Isaac spoke to Abraham his father and said, "My father!" And he said, "Here I am, my son." And he said, "Behold, the fire and the wood, but where is the lamb for the burnt offering?" And Abraham said, "God will provide for Himself the lamb for the burnt offering, my son." So the two of them walked on together. (Gen. 22:6–8)

"God will provide" . . . in this compassionate and hope-filled answer, we find the third facet of Abraham's response: it was *based on the character of God.* God had promised that, through Isaac, Abraham's descendants would be named (21:12), so this obedient father was staking his whole future on his Lord's unchangeable nature.

The fourth characteristic of Abraham's response was that it was *thorough and complete.* Just look at all of the preparations he carried out: he "saddled his donkey," "split wood" (22:3); "took the wood," "took in his hand the fire and the knife" (v. 6); "built the altar," "arranged the wood," "bound his son Isaac," "laid him on the altar" (v. 9); "stretched out his hand," and "took the knife to slay his son" (v. 10). His obedience didn't shrink from a single detail. And God rewarded him for his unflinching faith.

Reward of God

With his son Isaac, his only son, whom he loved, bound and waiting on the altar, Abraham raised the knife to plunge it into the boy, when suddenly

> the angel of the Lord called to him from heaven, and said, "Abraham, Abraham!"[4]

Though he had come to that place in his walk with God where He meant more to him than Isaac, Abraham nevertheless must have cried out hoarsely, "Here I am," with a mixture of relief and strained waiting to see what God would do next (v. 11b).

---

4. In Hebrew, when a name is repeated it is done so out of respect. This was as if God were saying, "I have no further need of proof. You have validated your faith."

What God did next was to reward Abraham with the life of his son.

> "Do not stretch out your hand against the lad, and do nothing to him; for now I know that you fear God, since you have not withheld your son, your only son, from Me." (v. 12)

Notice the phrase, "Now I know that you fear God." God was telling Abraham that he had indeed proved his faith, that he was more than a convert now; he had become a true servant.

So now we have seen two of Abraham's rewards: his son was spared and his obedience was approved. But there is one more. A substitute was given, fulfilling Abraham's trust that God would provide.

> Then Abraham raised his eyes and looked, and behold, behind him a ram caught in the thicket by his horns; and Abraham went and took the ram, and offered him up for a burnt offering in the place of his son. (v. 13)

How Abraham's heart must have overflowed with praise and adoration for his trustworthy Lord! He was so moved by God's provision that he

> called the name of that place The Lord Will Provide, as it is said to this day, "In the mount of the Lord it will be provided." (v. 14)

And Abraham's exultation did not go unnoticed by God.

> Then the angel of the Lord called to Abraham a second time from heaven, and said, "By Myself I have sworn, declares the Lord, because you have done this thing, and have not withheld your son, your only son, indeed I will greatly bless you, and I will greatly multiply your seed as the stars of the heavens, and as the sand which is on the seashore; and your seed shall possess the gate of their enemies. And in your seed all the nations of the earth shall be blessed, because you have obeyed My voice." So Abraham returned to his young men, and they arose and went together to Beersheba; and Abraham lived at Beersheba. (vv. 15–19)

Lessons for Our Learning

From this wonderful story of obedience we can glean at least three lessons.

First: *What you retain for yourself, God will ask you to release to Him.* It was the late Corrie ten Boom who said, "I've learned that we must hold everything loosely, because when I grip it tightly, it hurts when the Father pries my fingers loose and takes it from me!"[5] Whatever we try to keep for ourselves—whether our children, parents, position, or some cherished dream for our future—God wants us to lay that before Him, trusting Him with what is most dear and precious to us. And He is worthy of that trust, as the next lesson reveals.

Second: *What you release to God, He will replace with something better.* The replacement may not always come as quickly as Abraham's did, but it will come (compare Eccles. 11:1).

Third: *Whenever God replaces, He also rewards.* Rewarding is a part of God's very nature. Remember what the writer of Hebrews tells us? "He is a rewarder of those who seek Him" (11:6b). But He cannot reward when we will not release and allow Him to replace, as poet Martha Snell Nicholson illustrates.

> One by one He took them from me,
> All the things I valued most,
> Until I was empty-handed;
> Every glittering toy was lost,
>
> And I walked earth's highways, grieving,
> In my rags and poverty.
> Till I heard His voice inviting,
> "Lift your empty hands to Me!"
>
> So I held my hands toward Heaven,
> And He filled them with a store
> Of His own transcendent riches
> Till they could contain no more.
>
> And at last I comprehended
> With my stupid mind and dull,

---

5. As quoted by Charles R. Swindoll in *Living Above the Level of Mediocrity* (Waco, Tex.: Word Books Publisher, 1987), p. 114.

That God COULD not pour His riches
Into hands already full![6]

God needs the open hands of a convert in order to manufacture
a serving saint. Are you willing to open *your* hands to Him?

☕ *Living Insights*   STUDY ONE

Abraham's obedience was characterized by an immediate
response: faith, trust in God's character, and thoroughness. When
you hold your obedience up to Abraham's, how well does it match
his model? What do you see as your strengths?

_____

_____

_____

How about your weaknesses? Is there a particular aspect that
needs improvement?

_____

_____

_____

Why do you think obeying is easier for you in certain aspects
than in others? For example, what is motivating you in your strong
areas and hindering you in your weaker ones?

Stronger areas: _____

_____

_____

Weaker areas: _____

_____

_____

6. Martha Snell Nicholson, "Treasures," in *Ivory Palaces* (Wilmington, Calif.: Martha Snell
Nicholson, 1946), p. 67.

In today's lesson we surveyed four crises in Abraham's life, studying the final crisis in some detail. Let's take a few minutes now to shift the focus from Abraham's life to yours.

As you survey your life, list a few of the major crises you have endured.

1. _____

2. _____

3. _____

What aspect of your obedience was challenged in each of these crises?

1. _____

_____

2. _____

_____

3. _____

_____

Of those crises, which was the most difficult for you to face? Why?

_____

_____

_____

In what ways has this crisis strengthened your obedience to Christ?

_____

_____

_____

_____

Chapter 16

THE CONSEQUENCES OF SERVING

2 Corinthians 4:8–9; 11:22–28

Years ago, Americans devotedly watched a TV program called "Truth or Consequences." For those of you who never saw it, the format of the show was quite simple. The host, Bob Barker, would introduce a contestant who was then asked a question and given a set amount of time in which to answer. If the answer was correct—the "truth"—then a prize was given. If the answer was incorrect or not given in time, however, the contestant would have to suffer "consequences" that ranged from one ridiculous extreme to another.

Perhaps one of the reasons for the popularity of the program, aside from hilarious "consequences," is that viewers sensed a familiar parallel with life. Generally speaking, our society is built on the idea of rewarding what is true or good and punishing what is false or bad. Take driving, for example. If you stay within the speed limit and obey the other traffic rules, you are rewarded with the privilege of driving whenever and wherever you want. But if you hurtle down the highway and put others at risk, you get punished with a ticket or even lose your license.

Rewarding what's good and punishing what's bad makes sense. It's fair; it's what we want life to be like. Unfortunately, as all too many of us already know, life is not always logical or fair . . . not even for gentle, humble servants.

A Realistic Appraisal of Serving

The truth is, in the lives of all servants there will be times of reaping negative consequences for speaking the truth or for doing what is right. It happens, and it seems to be happening more frequently as society moves further and further away from the Lord. Just as Paul wrote in Romans 1, the ungodly suppress the truth—and along with that truth, all servants who model it (v. 18).

Enduring unfair consequences can be one of the most difficult tests any of us ever faces. Perhaps that's why the apostle Peter was moved by the Holy Spirit to give us two important reasons for patiently bearing such times. The first reason, found in 1 Peter 2, may surprise you.

> Servants, be submissive to your masters with all respect, not only to those who are good and gentle, but also to those who are unreasonable. For this finds favor, if for the sake of conscience toward God a man bears up under sorrows when suffering unjustly. For what credit is there if, when you sin and are harshly treated, you endure it with patience? But if when you do what is right and suffer for it you patiently endure it, this finds favor with God. (vv. 18–20)

Naturally, when we are punished instead of praised for doing good, we feel outraged. And that anger motivates us to defend ourselves, to discredit our accuser, to demand justice. The Lord, however, says that when we do just the opposite and humbly endure, we catch His eye, His heart, and His favor.

The second reason Peter encourages us to respond this way is that in doing so we follow Christ's example.

> For you have been called for this purpose, since Christ also suffered for you, leaving you an example for you to follow in His steps, who committed no sin, nor was any deceit found in His mouth; and while being reviled, He did not revile in return; while suffering, He uttered no threats, but kept entrusting Himself to Him who judges righteously. (vv. 21–23)

None of us will ever outgrow the need to follow Jesus' example. We will never reach a spiritual plateau where unfair treatment doesn't exist. If anything, the more committed and Christlike we become, the more we'll encounter this particular trial.

Paul certainly found this to be true. Rather than provide protection, his faithful ministry as a bond servant of the Lord constantly exposed him to mistreatment. If we turn to 2 Corinthians 4, we'll enter the dark, back-alley consequences he faced that are common to all servants.

The "Dark Side" of Serving

The fact that servants often suffer unjustly was not something Paul tried to hide from the Christians in Corinth. On the contrary, as you may recall from chapter 13, the Apostle vividly portrayed this dark side of serving in 2 Corinthians 4:8–9. He said he was "afflicted" in every way, meaning pressured, harassed, oppressed. He felt confused, "perplexed," "without resources, embarrassed, in doubt."[1] He was "persecuted," driven, kept on the run by the relentless pursuit of his enemies. And he was "struck down," a phrase whose meaning can be summed up in one word—*rejected*. It's as if he was identifying four broad categories of consequences all servants will be called upon to endure.

A little later in his letter, in chapter 11, Paul goes even further to give specific, personal examples of suffering from each of the four categories. Why? To combat all the negative things the false apostles were saying about his authority and authenticity as a servant. Listen as he begins his defense:

> Are they Hebrews? So am I. Are they Israelites? So
> am I. Are they descendants of Abraham? So am I.
> Are they servants of Christ? (I speak as if insane.)
> (vv. 22–23a)

With rapid-fire questions, Paul compares himself to his critics while working his way up to the key issue of his servanthood. In a parenthetical aside, he tells us just how absurd he feels in making this comparison, but he does so for the sake of the Corinthians.

"Are they servants?" Paul asks, "I more so." And he goes on to present the evidence. But it's not what we might expect. Instead of describing all his wonderful achievements, he chronicles his sufferings—which have interesting parallels with the categories from chapter 4.

> In far more labors, in far more imprisonments,
> beaten times without number, often in danger of
> death. (v. 23b)

In Far More Labors

The Greek word for "labors" used here is *kopos*, meaning "personal toil, trouble, painful effort, stress to the point of exhaustion." Although a different term from the one Paul used in chapter 4 for "afflicted," it still communicates the same idea. Paul makes this

---

1. W. E. Vine, *Vine's Expository Dictionary of New Testament Words* (McClean, Va.: MacDonald Publishing Co., n.d.), p. 336.

even clearer as he describes some of the conditions under which he labored.

> I have been in labor and hardship, through many sleepless nights, in hunger and thirst, often without food, in cold and exposure. Apart from such external things, there is the daily pressure upon me of concern for all the churches. (11:27–28)

Many of us have created such a stained-glass image of Paul that we forget that he wrestled with the same afflictions of servanthood we do. The sleepless nights, the hunger, the pressure—this all came as a direct result of his laying down his life to serve others.

In Far More Imprisonments

Paul's prison experiences answer to the second category: confusion, embarrassment, doubt, and being without any resources.

> I have been on frequent journeys, in dangers from rivers, dangers from robbers, dangers from my countrymen, dangers from the Gentiles, dangers in the city, dangers in the wilderness, dangers on the sea, dangers among false brethren. (v. 26)

In this one verse, Paul uses "dangers," *kindunos*, eight times. Everywhere the Apostle went, dangers abounded. Having to live with such constant peril could easily have caused him to wonder about the Lord's goodness. Who could fault him for crying, "Lord, why should someone who faithfully serves you live like a hunted animal? This isn't fair!"

As servants, though, we are called to live transparent, vulnerable lives, which can sometimes leave us open to danger and uncertainty. And when life is shaky and we're feeling insecure, it's easy to begin feeling that our confusion and doubts are inescapable.

Beaten Times without Number

The reality of our third category, persecution, is never clearer or more repugnant than when it involves physical abuse. "Five times I received from the Jews thirty-nine lashes. Three times I was beaten with rods, once I was stoned" (vv. 24–25a). Who said that, a crook? A murderer? No, a servant. And Paul was not alone. Many servants have experienced such persecution. If you doubt that, just read *Fox's Book of Martyrs* or Richard Wurmbrand's *Tortured for Christ* or *A*

Spoke in the Wheel (Renate Wind's captivating biography of Dietrich Bonhoeffer) or Corrie ten Boom's *The Hiding Place*.

Often in Danger of Death

The phrase "in danger of death" implies that, though deadly enemies were hot on his heels, Paul was still a step ahead of them—death had not overtaken him yet (v. 23). In this we can see a link to chapter 4, where Paul said he was "struck down, but not destroyed" (v. 9). Just how often Paul was struck down and how close he came to being destroyed is revealed in chapter 11:

- Shipwrecked three times (v. 25)

- A day and a night spent in the ocean (v. 25)

- Surrounded by constant dangers (v. 26)

- Without sufficient food (v. 27)

- Being exposed to the elements (v. 27)

- Eluding death through a daring escape (v. 33)

Suggestions for Coping with Consequences

As servants, how do we cope with the harsh reality of mistreatment? What can help us endure?

Two reassuring truths to hold on to during unsettling times are, first, *nothing touches us that hasn't passed through the hands of our heavenly Father. Nothing.* Whatever mistreatment occurs, we can bear up under it with the courage and confidence that comes from knowing that it has first been sovereignly surveyed and permitted by our Lord.

Second, *everything we endure is designed to prepare us for serving others more effectively. Everything.* Paul affirms this same truth in the opening to his second letter to the Corinthians:

> Thank God, the Father of our Lord Jesus Christ, that he is our Father and the source of all mercy and comfort. For he gives us comfort in all our trials so that we in turn may be able to give the same sort of strong sympathy to others in their troubles that we receive from God. (1:3–4 PHILLIPS)

When we have realistically faced and endured dark times of

unfair consequences, we can better understand and serve those who face similar struggles.

Living Insights

We've looked at some personal examples of unjust suffering from the apostle Paul's life; now let's examine a few in our own. Under each of the four categories from our study, write down any specific experiences you've endured.

Affliction _____

_____

_____

Confusion _____

_____

_____

Persecution _____

_____

_____

Rejection _____

_____

_____

As Paul writes in 2 Corinthians 1:3–7, God comforts each of us in our sufferings so that we might minister effectively to others who experience similar trials. With that in mind, think back to the most difficult mistreatment you've suffered and how God comforted you during that time. Is a close friend experiencing a similar consequence? What counsel could you give this other person? How could you offer comfort?

_____

_____

Alexander Solzhenitsyn and Elie Wiesel. Both men represent millions of other men, women, and children who have been imprisoned and forgotten by man. People who suffered unjustly in Russian gulags or Nazi concentration camps. For some, like Solzhenitsyn, these man-made hells helped bring about their spiritual conversion. For others, like Wiesel, the hellish experience reduced what faith they had to a scorched cinder.

> Never shall I forget that night, the first night in camp, which has turned my life into one long night, seven times cursed and seven times sealed. Never shall I forget that smoke. Never shall I forget the little faces of the children, whose bodies I saw turned into wreaths of smoke beneath a silent blue sky.
>
> Never shall I forget those flames which consumed my faith forever.
>
> Never shall I forget that nocturnal silence which deprived me, for all eternity, of the desire to live. Never shall I forget those moments which murdered my God and my soul and turned my dreams to dust. Never shall I forget these things, even if I am condemned to live as long as God Himself. Never.

The pain of suffering unjustly is one of the severest trials we can enter into. It is a sanctuary of flames from which some emerge with a tempered, unshakable faith; while others, only ashes.[2]

---

2. Lee Hough, from the study guide *Joseph: From Pit to Pinnacle*, from the Bible-teaching ministry of Charles R. Swindoll (Fullerton, Calif.: Insight for Living, 1990), p. 19. Elie Wiesel is quoted from *Night*, trans. Stella Rodway (New York, N.Y.: Bantam Books, 1960), p. 32.

Perhaps your faith is being refined in the fire of unjust suffering right now. The persecution and pain are intense. What is it that can protect your faith from being consumed?

The greatest test in this kind of suffering is our attitude toward it. Viktor Frankl wrote,

> Everything can be taken from a man but one thing: the last of the human freedoms—to choose one's attitude in any given set of circumstances, to choose one's own way.

We cannot control whether today or tomorrow we will be treated fairly. But we can choose how we will respond. Our attitude is something we can control.[3]

What attitude have you chosen in response to your situation? Is it one that encourages you to patiently endure?

What attitude did Jesus choose when He was treated unfairly? Read 1 Peter 2:21–23. How might this same attitude enable you to endure?

_____

_____

_____

_____

_____

3. Hough, *Joseph*, p. 20. Viktor E. Frankl is quoted from *Man's Search for Meaning*, rev. ed. (New York, N.Y.: Pocket Books, 1984), p. 86.

Chapter 17

THE REWARDS OF SERVING

Selected Scriptures

Jesus assures us that

> "not one sparrow (What do they cost? Two for a penny?) can fall to the ground without your Father knowing it." (Matt. 10:29 LB)

Neither will He miss knowing how you faithfully mow your disabled neighbor's yard each week. He saw you deliver food on that needy family's porch during the night. He watched as you quietly, humbly reached out to restore the brother who strayed. He noticed when you selflessly volunteered to do the behind-the-scenes job no one else wanted.

Not one act of servanthood, no matter how small or seemingly insignificant, can fall to the ground without our Father knowing it. Others may miss what we do; they may forget how we went the extra mile; they may even belittle our acts of kindness. But not our Father in heaven.

He sees . . .

He remembers . . .

And He promises to reward.

Some General Facts about Rewards

To gain a broader understanding of rewards, let's examine several passages of Scripture, beginning with 1 Corinthians 3.

> According to the grace of God which was given to me, as a wise master builder I laid a foundation, and another is building upon it. But let each man be careful how he builds upon it. For no man can lay a foundation other than the one which is laid, which is Jesus Christ. Now if any man builds upon the foundation with gold, silver, precious stones, wood, hay, straw, each man's work will become evident; for the day will show it, because it is to be

revealed with fire; and the fire itself will test the quality of each man's work. If any man's work which he has built upon it remains, he shall receive a reward. (vv. 10–14)

Looking closely, we can extract from this passage three important truths concerning rewards. First: *Most rewards are received in heaven, not on earth* (v. 13a). The "day" that Paul refers to here is the Judgment Day.[1] Second: *All rewards are based on quality, not quantity* (v. 13b). It isn't the size, volume, noise, or number of our works that impresses God; it is our heart's motive and authenticity. And third: *No reward that is postponed will be forgotten* (v. 14). As servants, we all will minister at times without recognition. But that's not to say that our good works will never be rewarded.

> God doesn't settle His accounts at the end of every day. Nor does He close out His books toward the end of everyone's life. No, not then. But be assured, fellow servant, when that day in eternity dawns, when time shall be no more on this earth, no act of serving others—be it well-known or unknown by others—will be forgotten.[2]

God's Promises to Servants

We can count on our rewards because we can count on God's promises. He always keeps His word—a truth that can keep us going when we hit hard times. We can divide His promises into two groups: those dealing with His faithfulness and those dealing with His recognition of ours.

Regarding His Faithfulness

To understand why we can rest assured that no reward will be forgotten, let's turn now to Hebrews 6:10.

> For God is not unjust so as to forget your work and the love which you have shown toward His name, in having ministered and in still ministering to the saints.

1. See 2 Thessalonians 1:10; 2 Timothy 1:12, 18; 4:8; 1 Peter 2:12; 1 John 4:17.

2. Charles R. Swindoll, *Improving Your Serve: The Art of Unselfish Living* (Waco, Tex.: Word Books Publisher, 1981), p. 195.

The context indicates that the writer is addressing Christians.

> The word *beloved* in the previous verse assures us of
> that. And he is writing out of concern for a few of
> the first-century believers who had begun to cool off
> and drift from a close walk with God. He wants to
> encourage them to stay at it, to keep going, to count
> on the Lord their God to take notice of them and
> reward them accordingly. In other words, he reminds
> them of that great truth all of us tend to forget when
> days turn into a slow grind, *God is faithful!*[3]

What specifically do we mean when we speak of God's faithfulness? That He is steadfast in His allegiance to His people. That He is firm about fulfilling His promises. That there are no ups and downs, no hot and cold with God; He's always dependable, loyal, constant, and steady.

Hebrews 6:10 tells us more than just that, however. We also learn that the Lord demonstrates His faithfulness toward us in two ways:

1. He remembers our work—each individual act.
2. He takes note of the love that prompted us to act.

How can we know that a reward that is postponed will not be forgotten? Because God is faithful. And because He is faithful, the writer of Hebrews encourages his readers and all servants to remain steadfast.

> And we desire that each one of you show the same
> diligence so as to realize the full assurance of hope
> until the end, that you may not be sluggish, but
> imitators of those who through faith and patience
> inherit the promises. (vv. 11–12)

Regarding Our Faithfulness

In addition to those promises about His own faithfulness, God has also made certain promises to His servants regarding their faithfulness. For example,

> Therefore, my beloved brethren, be steadfast, im-
> movable, always abounding in the work of the Lord,

---

3. Swindoll, *Improving Your Serve*, pp. 198–99.

143

knowing that your toil is *not in vain* in the Lord.
(1 Cor. 15:58, emphasis added)

And let us not lose heart in doing good, for in due
time *we shall reap* if we do not grow weary. So then,
while we have opportunity, let us do good to all men,
and especially to those who are of the household of
the faith. (Gal. 6:9–10, emphasis added)

With good will render service, as to the Lord, and
not to men, knowing that whatever good thing each
one does, this *he will receive back* from the Lord,
whether slave or free. (Eph. 6:7–8, emphasis added)

When you've done what was needed and were ignored, you can
be sure it was "not in vain." When you did what was right with the
right motive but received no credit, not even a "thank you," God
promises you "shall reap." When you voluntarily assumed the role
of a servant and washed another person's feet, you "will receive
back." But how, exactly? When?

God's reward system has both a temporal and an eternal side to
it. For a look at the temporal, turn back to the familiar passage of
2 Corinthians 4. Following closely on the heels of the "painful" side
of servanthood, Paul mentions some rewards as well.

We always carry around in our body the death of
Jesus, so that the life of Jesus may also be revealed
in our body. For we who are alive are always being
given over to death for Jesus' sake, so that his life
may be revealed in our mortal body. (vv. 10–11 NIV)

One temporal reward reflected in Paul's words is *the quiet awareness that the life of Christ is being modeled.* Few things bring a greater
sense of satisfaction than knowing that our actions and motives
manifest Christ. One other temporal reward mentioned in this same
chapter is found in verse 15.

For all things are for your sakes, that the grace which
is spreading to more and more people may cause the
giving of thanks to abound to the glory of God.

When we serve, *we reap the joyful realization that a thankful spirit
is being stimulated,* both in ourselves and in others.

As for our eternal rewards, one will be the satisfaction of being commended by Jesus in the same manner the king commends his servants in the parable of Matthew 25:14–30: "Well done, good and faithful [servant]; you were faithful with a few things, I will put you in charge of many things; enter into the joy of your master" (v. 21).

Another eternal reward will be receiving crowns. Five are mentioned in the New Testament. In 1 Corinthians 9:24–27, there is the *imperishable crown* given to those who victoriously run the race of life. In Philippians 4:1 and 1 Thessalonians 2:19–20 is the *crown of exultation*. It is reserved for those servants who faithfully evangelize and disciple others. In 2 Timothy 4:7–8 there is the *crown of righteousness*, which will be awarded to all who live each day in anticipation of Christ's return. In James 1:12 is the *crown of life*, the wonderful reward for those who endure suffering and trials, all the while continuing to love the Savior. And in 1 Peter 5:1–4 is the *crown of glory*, promised to those who faithfully shepherd God's flock.

Concluding Encouragements to Servants

We've traveled a long and sometimes arduous road in our journey into servanthood, covering the pristine territory of unselfishness, the wide plains of forgiveness, the pinnacles of influence, and the treacherous descents of perils and consequences. The journey is not through, however, and the best land, as we've seen from this lesson, is up ahead.

As we pack up our thoughts, take these three servant supplies with you for encouragement along your way:

- God takes notice of every act of servanthood.

- When God takes notice, He especially observes the heart.

- A servant's heart remains one of the rarest jewels on earth.

🍵 *Living Insights* STUDY ONE

Take some time to expand your understanding of rewards by examining the following passages. As you read them, let these questions spur your thinking: What do rewards teach you about God? How do they hone your eternal perspective on life? What about them gives you hope? Jot down your insights and observations in the space provided.

Psalm 19:7–11 _____

_____

Psalm 127:3 _____

_____

Proverbs 11:18 _____

_____

Proverbs 25:21–22 _____

_____

Matthew 5:10–12 _____

_____

Matthew 6:1–18 _____

_____

Matthew 10:41–42 _____

_____

1 Corinthians 3:8 _____

_____

Hebrews 11:6 _____

_____

Hebrew 11:24–26 _____

_____

🍺 *Living Insights* STUDY TWO

What is the Teacher doing? Only the splashes and trickles of water from dripping feet echo through the silent Upper Room—no profound or puzzling words of explanation come from Jesus' lips.

After a brief confrontation with Peter, Jesus is silent again, letting His message be told through the quiet voice of water and towel.

Finally done, He sits back and looks intently into the disciples' eyes . . . and ours. "Do you know what I have done?" He asks. At this point in our study, we surely do know. Jesus has showed us the essence of humble, gentle service. Then, "if you know these things," He adds, "you are blessed if you do them" (John 13:3–17).

Will you take the towel and basin Jesus is extending to you now? You will be blessed if you do what you learn. Jesus has promised.

In the space provided, write down just one thing you have learned from each chapter and how you plan to apply it.

Who, Me a Servant? You Gotta Be Kidding! _____

_____

God's Work, My Involvement _____

_____

A Case for Unselfishness _____

_____

The Servant as a Giver (Part One) _____

_____

The Servant as a Giver (Part Two) _____

_____

The Servant as a Forgiver (Part One) _____

_____

The Servant as a Forgiver (Part Two) _____

_____

The Servant as a Forgetter _____

_____

Thinking like a Servant Thinks _____

BOOKS FOR PROBING FURTHER

For those of you who want to learn more about developing and expressing a servant's heart, we recommend the following resources.

Christ, the Servant's Example

Gire, Ken. *Intimate Moments with the Savior: Learning to Love.* Grand Rapids, Mich.: Zondervan Publishing House, 1989.

————. *Incredible Moments with the Savior: Learning to See.* Grand Rapids, Mich.: Zondervan Publishing House, 1990.

————. *Instructive Moments with the Savior: Learning to Hear.* Grand Rapids, Mich.: Zondervan Publishing House, 1992.

Griffiths, Michael. *The Example of Jesus.* The Jesus Library series. Downers Grove, Ill.: InterVarsity Press, 1985.

Strauss, Richard L. *Growing More like Jesus.* Neptune, N.J.: Loizeaux Brothers, 1991.

The Servant's Spirit: Giving, Forgiving, and Forgetting

Campolo, Tony, and Gordon Aeschliman. *50 Ways You Can Feed a Hungry World.* Downers Grove, Ill.: InterVarsity Press, 1991.

Ronsvalle, John and Sylvia. *The Poor Have Faces.* Grand Rapids, Mich.: Baker Book House, 1992.

Smedes, Lewis B. *Forgive and Forget: Healing the Hurts We Don't Deserve.* New York, N.Y.: Pocket Books, 1984.

Stoop, David, and James Masteller. *Forgiving Our Parents, Forgiving Ourselves.* Ann Arbor, Mich.: Servant Publications, Vine Books, 1991.

Portrait of a Servant: The Beatitudes

Barclay, William. *The Gospel of Matthew.* Vol. 1. Rev. ed. The Daily Study Bible Series. Philadelphia, Pa.: Westminster Press, 1975.

Stott, John R. W. *The Message of the Sermon on the Mount (Matthew 5–7: Christian Counter-Culture.* Downers Grove, Ill.: Inter-Varsity Press, 1978.

The Servant's Influence: Salt and Light

Collins, Gary R. *You Can Make a Difference: 14 Principles for Influencing Lives.* Grand Rapids, Mich.: Zondervan Publishing House, 1992.

Colson, Charles, with Ellen Santilli Vaughn. *The Body: Being Light in Darkness.* Dallas, Tex.: Word Publishing, 1992.

D'Arcy, Paula. *When Your Friend Is Grieving: Building a Bridge of Love.* Wheaton, Ill.: Harold Shaw Publishers, 1990.

Prior, David. *Creating Community.* Colorado Springs, Colo.: Nav-Press, 1992.

The Servant's Thinking and Obedience

Taylor, Daniel. *The Myth of Certainty: Trusting God, Asking Questions, Taking Risks.* Grand Rapids, Mich.: Zondervan Publishing House, 1992.

Thatcher, Martha. *The Freedom of Obedience.* The Christian Character Library series. Colorado Springs, Colo.: NavPress, 1986.

Servanthood

Fleming, Kenneth C. *He Humbled Himself: Recovering the Lost Art of Serving.* Westchester, Ill.: Good News Publishers, Crossway Books, 1989.

Price, Nelson L. *Servants, Not Celebrities.* Nashville, Tenn.: Broadman Press, 1989.

Swindoll, Charles R. *Improving Your Serve.* Waco, Tex.: Word Books Publishers, 1981.

Some of these books may be out of print and available only through a library. For those currently available, please contact your local Christian bookstore. Books by Charles R. Swindoll may be obtained through Insight for Living. IFL also offers some books by other authors—please note the ordering information that follows and contact the office that serves you.

ACKNOWLEDGMENTS

Insight for Living is grateful to the sources below for permission to use their material.

Barclay, William. *The Gospel of Matthew.* Vol. 1. Rev. ed. The Daily Study Bible Series. Philadelphia, Pa.: Westminster Press, 1975. Used by kind permission of The Saint Andrew Press, Edinburgh, Scotland.

Calkin, Ruth Harms. "I Wonder," in *Tell Me Again, Lord, I Forget.* Wheaton, Ill.: Tyndale House Publishers, 1974. Used by permission.

Colson, Charles W., with Ellen Santilli Vaughn. *The Body: Being Light in Darkness.* Dallas, Tex.: Word Publishing, 1992. Used by permission.

Swindoll, Charles R. *Improving Your Serve.* Dallas, Tex.: Word Books, 1981. Used by permission.

Ten Boom, Corrie, with John and Elizabeth Sherrill. *The Hiding Place.* Chappaqua, N.Y.: Chosen Books, Inc., 1971. Used by permission.

NOTES

NOTES